D1796811

WHO'S GOING TO LOOK AT YOU?

WHO'S GOING TO
LOOK AT YOU?

Mark Eden

Matador
5 Weir Road
Kibworth Beauchamp
Leicester LE8 0LQ, UK
Tel: (+44) 116 279 2299
Fax: (+44) 116 279 2277
Email: books@troubador.co.uk
Web: www.troubador.co.uk/matador

ISBN 978 1848765 337

British Library Cataloguing in Publication Data.
A catalogue record for this book is available from the British Library.

Typeset in 11.5pt Palatino by Troubador Publishing Ltd, Leicester, UK
Printed in the UK by TJ International, Padstow, Cornwall

Matador is an imprint of Troubador Publishing Ltd

To my darling Sue.
Without whom my life story
would not have had such a happy ending.

Foreword

I have never kept a diary; probably because I never thought my life would be anything to write home about, let alone write a book about. So I have had to rely mainly on memory which, as we know, can sometimes deceive us. However in writing this memoir I have been surprised by how much I *do* remember, especially from my childhood in the 1930's, which coincided with two seismic events; the Great Depression and the beginning of World War Two. I have written this memoir primarily for my children, my grand children and even my great-grandchildren; so that they would know a little about the life and times of one of their forefathers. However should *you*, dear reader, decide to buy this book you will be making an old man very happy; and at the same time help to keep the wolf from the door of my dotage!

Mark Eden. 82½.

ACKNOWLEDGEMENTS

Grateful thanks to my friend Stafford Hildred for his enthusiasm, guidance and support in the preparation and publishing of this book. I would also like to thank Stewart Darby for the cover picture and some of the photographs of Sue and I in the picture section, and Roger Langley, author of the excellent book, *Patrick McGoohan: Danger Man or Prisoner*.

Oft in the stilly night,
Ere slumber's chain has bound me,
Fond memory brings the light
Of other days around me;
The smiles, the tears,
Of boyhood years,
The words of love then spoken;
The eyes that shone,
Now dimm'd and gone,
The cheerful hearts now broken!

Thomas Moore.

CHAPTER 1

THE BOYHOOD YEARS

"In the dark womb where I began,
My mother's life made me a man."

Me and Mickey Mouse are the same age! Looking back, 1928 may not have been a momentous year but it had its moments. In America Herbert.C.Hoover was elected President. Gene Tunney retired as undefeated Heavyweight Champion of the World. Walter Deamer invented bubble-gum, and the aforementioned Mickey Mouse made his screen debut in Walt Disney's 'Steamboat Willy'. In Britain the Equal Franchise Bill was passed, giving all women over the age of 21 the vote. Alexander Fleming discovered Penicillin. Thomas Hardy died and Blackburn Rovers won the FA Cup.

It was on St. Valentine's Day of that year, at around 8.30pm that I made my first entrance - at 165 Stanhope Street in the (then) borough of St.Pancras in London. As births go, mine would be classified as 'humble'. Coming into the world in the gas-lit top back room of a tenement house in one of the poorest areas of London could hardly be described as anything else. We had no running water and no sink. There was a cold water tap on the landing two flights down, and the lavatory was out in the back yard and shared by three families. With my birth imminent my father hastily contacted our landlady, Mrs Nicola who lived in the basement, who then went to the pub on the corner to summon the local midwife. Mrs Nicola was a widow who, in common with the legions of women whose husbands had 'fallen' in The First World War, always wore black in lifelong mourning for the men who had marched off to battle and never returned.

In spite of everything (my mother swore the midwife was drunk!) I was safely delivered, weighing in at just over eight pounds, and welcomed into a loving but poverty-stricken, Catholic working-class family. My father was 28; my mother was 25, and my brother Eddie 3. According to my mother, they had had three years of 'purgatory' with my elder brother. He was, in my mother's words, a 'real handful', hyper-active, mischievous, and never seemed to need sleep. Imagine their relief then when I came along; good natured, slept all the time, and never cried.

Our family name is Malin, and in the March of that year, at St Aloysius Catholic church in Somers Town, I was baptized Douglas John.

I was named Douglas, believe it or not, after Field Marshal Douglas Haig, Commander-in-Chief of British forces in the First World War.

Haig was the brilliant military tactician who devised the strategy of pounding the German lines with heavy artillery fire all night, to let them know we were planning an attack the next morning, and then at dawn sending wave upon wave of young conscripts walking slowly across no-man's-land, with sixty pound packs on their backs, into devastating German machine gun fire. Sustaining immense loss of life grotesquely out of all proportion to any ground gained. Ground that, more often than not, would be retaken in the next German counter attack. To my parents however (and to many others) he was a hero. The fact that he was an obdurate, incompetent soldier who had twice failed his entrance examination to Sandhurst, and was only accepted after the personal intervention of King George V, was not to become widely known until sometime later.

My mother's maiden name was Tompkins. She was born in Reading Berkshire, on the 26th of March 1903, and was baptized Emma Marguerite; but for some unaccountable reason was known all her life as 'Mag'. She died on the 6th of June 2003, ten weeks after reaching her 100th birthday. An indomitable, courageous, saintly woman who, if there *is* a Heaven, has most surely attained her place in it, on the top table! When she was 11 years old her beloved mother died, and she was inconsolable. Within a year her father had remarried. Her stepmother, a stony-faced widow with two daughters of her own, soon made it clear that she had no intention of looking after another five children. To his eternal shame my mother's father acquiesced and stood meekly by as, one by one, they were off-loaded. One brother was sent to a Naval Training school and the two others were found jobs that provided live-in accommodation. Her elder sister went off to join distant relatives in Canada and, at the tender age of 12, unwanted, unloved and forlorn, my mother was put into service as a scullery maid. Because they all lived in Berkshire and seldom visited London, I never really knew my mother's side of the family, so I shall leave it at that. The name Malin is Irish. The spelling and pronunciation are the same as Malin Head in County Donegal. There was also a William Malin who was executed by the British for his part in the Easter uprising in 1916, so I assume my grandfather was of Irish descent.

I say 'assume' because he was born in a Workhouse and for a short while attended the Ragged School, but the necessity of having to earn a living forced him to leave and take on any work that came his way. When he was 14 years old he stood up to his drunken, violent father and, after a fierce fight, threw him out of the house and took on the responsibility of bread-winner for the family. He became a scaffolder, more often than not rising at dawn to walk to work in order to save the tram fare. My paternal grandmother's maiden name was Ellis; she was born in Cork in southern Ireland and came over to England as a young girl. She was a big, strapping woman by all accounts. I remember my father telling me he once saw her take on a man in a fist fight and knock him out cold! When granddad met her he was virtually illiterate, and it was she who taught him to read and write.

In the W.C.Fields film My Little Chickadee, the great W.C. is sitting at a card table studying his hand when a stranger approaches. "Is this a game of chance?" he asks. W.C studies the sucker for a moment and says, "Not the way I play it." The same could be said for my grandfather, because he could manipulate a deck of cards, either by marking them or by sleight-of-hand, so that he would know what kind of hands the other players were holding. This meant, of course, that he couldn't lose. Among the kind of people with whom my grandfather mixed, cheating at cards was a high-risk venture. Stealing from your own kind was considered 'well out of order' bringing down grievous bodily harm on the perpetrator if discovered. Well aware of this, grandad would occasionally lose small sums, or come out even in an attempt to allay suspicion; nevertheless it remained a dangerous enterprise. One night he had been playing cards with three very tough characters, using his own marked deck. Two of the men were brothers, and it was in their rooms that the game was held. As was his custom, grandad had won enough for his immediate family needs, returned home and gone to bed. In the early hours of the morning he suddenly awoke with the heart-stopping realisation that he had left his pack of marked cards on the mantel shelf of the room in which they had been playing! Knowing that if either of the two brothers examined the cards too closely in daylight he could be spending the next three months in hospital, he got dressed, went back to the house, shinned up a drainpipe, opened a window and climbed inside.

The room in which they had been playing was the brothers' bedroom, and he had to tip-toe past their sleeping bodies to retrieve the incriminating pack of cards and make good his escape. When he got back home grandma was waiting for him and a furious row ensued.

She told him frankly that if he had ended up in hospital, there would have been no money coming in. No money coming in meant no rent. No rent meant eviction, and eviction would mean the workhouse for her and the children. Grandad didn't need much persuading. The events of that night had left him badly shaken, and from then on he never played cards for money again. In later life although he would delight his children with his card tricks, he would never show them how it was done, nor would he tell them the system he used to mark a deck of cards.

Grandma's death in 1912 at the early age of 38 left him devastated.

His 'old dutch' had been the bedrock of his life and now she was gone, leaving him with eight children (four boys and four girls) to bring up on his own. The eldest was 15, the youngest just 18 months. Apparently he had made two promises to his dying wife. The first was to do his utmost to keep the family together. Even today such an undertaking would be difficult; in 1912 it must have been virtually impossible. But in spite of the many seemingly insurmountable obstacles, he did it. The two eldest girls looked after the younger ones. The eldest son was already working, all the children helped out in some way, friends and neighbours rallied round, and the Malins stayed together. The second promise he had made was to continue bringing the children up in the Catholic religion. Although not a Catholic himself he made sure all the kids went to a Catholic school, attended Mass every Sunday, and kept all the observances of the Roman Church.

He was a real, old-fashioned cockney working man, my granddad: shrewd, funny, proud and down-to-earth.

Chill penury may have repressed his noble rage, but it never quenched his noble spirit. He always wore his cap, indoors or out; and in winter would always put on a scarf to 'go out the back', his euphemism for going to the lavatory. When his hair turned prematurely white he tried dying it with cold tea, leaving him with hair the colour of burnt orange! Not out of vanity, for he had none.

It was simply that work was hard to come by and, in a highly competitive labour market, white hair was a big disadvantage, especially in the building trade. Everyone who knew Frank Malin, admired and respected him, and his kids adored him. I just wish I could have got to know him better – and for longer. One last story about grandad; one which I think says a lot about him. In September 1940 he was on his death-bed. One evening, as the end drew near the assembled family sent for the parish priest to administer the last rites. When the priest came downstairs to talk to the family afterwards he was smiling to himself; and told them this story. Just before anointing him with Extreme Unction he said to granddad: "Is there anything you want to tell me?" Meaning, is there anything you want to confess? "Yes Father," he said. "I heard they're going to put another penny on the price of the working man's pint of beer. Isn't that a terrible thing?" He died early the next morning, more concerned about the cost of a pint than the price of salvation.

There was a little ditty he used to sing when he'd had a pint or two himself down at the Lincoln Arms in York Way. I assume it was a Music Hall song; although I have never heard it sung by anyone else, or come across a copy of it anywhere. Here it is as he would sing it in his ripe cockney accent.

> *Me and my pal were dustmen,*
> *Always worked the same old round.*
> *Strange to say we struck a Klondyke,*
> *Ought to see the wealf we found.*
> *'Apennies, pennies, farvins fousands,*
> *And to fink last week that I was poor.*
> *Oh, I'm goin' to be a regular Toff,*
> *Ridin' in me carriage and me pair.*
> *Top hat on me head, fevvers in me bed,*
> *Fink that I'm the Duke of Malboro' Fair.*
> *With me Astermadamcanda round the Marble Arch,*
> *A Piccadilly window in me eye*
> *Fancy all the dustmen shoutin' in yer ear,*
> *Leave us in yer will before you die.*

My father was born at 60 Wharfdale Road, King's Cross, on the third of September in 1900, and was christened Charles John. I know very little about his early life, except that it was hard. When he was eight years old he had been rushed to hospital with diphtheria and given a tracheotomy. This experience, coupled with the trauma of sitting by his mother's sick-bed, gave him a life-long aversion to hospitals and the smell of them; 'cabbage and carbolic' is how he described it. He had several jobs, one of which was driving a horse-drawn lorry for the old L.N.E.R at King's Cross station. When he was 18 he was called up for military service. Fortunately for him by the time he'd finished his training the War was over, and he spent three years with the army of occupation in Germany. Incidentally, my father had the dubious distinction of serving in both World Wars. When he was 42 he was called up again!

In the summer of 1923 my mother was working as a live-in housemaid in Lancaster Gate in SW London. One Sunday, on her only morning off, she and a girl friend went to church and then went for a walk in Kensington Gardens, where two young men got talking to them. One of them was my father-to-be. Nine months later, on March the 22nd 1924, they were married at St. Mark's Catholic Church in Reading (my mother having converted to the Catholic Faith). I've always been fascinated by the randomness of the events which shape our lives. The element of 'chance' in almost everything we do that defines our destiny. What if...my mother and her friend had gone for a walk in Hyde Park instead of Kensington Gardens? What if they had taken a different route to the one they took that morning? What if...?

The reception was held at my mother's family home, and there is a wonderful photograph of the wedding group taken in the back garden: my mother in her wedding dress looking radiantly beautiful, my father looking debonair and handsome, everyone done up to the nines...and her step-mother in her *pinafore*, which she had refused to take off. She is sitting at the end of the front row, half turned away from the camera, a look of stony disapproval writ large upon her unforgiving face. As far as I know, her own two daughters never married.

On the 28th of July 1930 my brother Charlie was born at St. Pancras Hospital in Somers Town. Because of pre-natal complications my mother had been admitted to hospital as a precautionary measure. When she came back with the new addition to the family, it meant that there were now five of us in two small rooms at the top of the house with no running water and no sink. Bit tricky that, with two small kids and a newly-born.

Our landlady Mrs Nicola was not an uncaring woman, but she could see that the status quo was not going to work. Consequently, after a few months, she regretfully informed my parents that, with the other tenants to consider, it would be better all round if we found somewhere else to live. Easier said than done! My dad was out of work at the time and his dole money was sixteen shillings (80p) a week.

After paying rent of seven shillings and sixpence there wasn't much left over for luxuries such as food and clothing; leaving aside the added expense of moving. Also, house owners were understandably reluctant to accept families such as ours, with the breadwinner on the dole and three children under the age of five. In the event we found somewhere cheaper, a whole sixpence a week cheaper, further down the same street at number 93. Insofar as there *was* a better end to Stanhope Street it was where we already were. Only 30 yards further up was Park Village East (very posh). Number 93 was towards the Euston Road end. Gulp! We were moving downmarket! The only upmarket thing about our new home was the eminence of its landlord: King George the Fifth! We were now living in Crown property, but no Grace and Favour apartment I can assure you. Having all been built around the same time the layout of number 93 was more or less the same as 165. (I didn't realise it at the time of course, but they were Georgian terraced houses; the kind that would fetch a small fortune today!) So nothing much had really changed except that we were now on the first floor, and in one room divided by folding doors. We still had no sink or running water. The cold water tap was only one flight down, but the lavatory was still out in the back yard and shared by three families. It was damp, there were bugs behind the wallpaper and mice behind the wainscot, but it was to be our home for the next eight years.

The only good thing about 'No-Hope' Street as Stanhope Street was called, was that just a few hundred yards away, on the other side of Albany Street, embraced by the majestic Nash Terraces, were the verdant acres of Regent's Park. It is impossible to overstate the importance of Regent's Park in our lives at that time, and most of the long summer days of my early childhood were spent there.

Almost every day during the school holidays my mother would cut us a pile of 'door-step' jam sandwiches, fill a lemonade bottle with water and off we would go; smacking our rumps as we urged our trusty steeds through the grimy, hard-cobbled streets up to the sun-lit plains of Regent's Park. Once there, plots would be hatched, ambushes laid, battles fought, friendships forged and enemies routed. Not until the sun began to dip towards the west would we homeward plod our weary way, to eat, sleep and gird our loins for more derring-do on the morrow. We would have been gone all day and never been in any danger, apart from the boisterous rough-and-tumble of our games.

Today's children have many things we could only dream of then, except perhaps the single most essential requirement of childhood – the freedom to roam unsupervised. Regent's Park was our playground. It had two sand-pits containing swings, see-saws and roundabouts. There were two boating lakes, bandstands, an open-air gymnasium and, of course, the Zoo. Apart from the boating lakes and the Zoo everything else was free; but even the Zoo was to become 'free' for us because we worked out a way to 'bunk in'. On one side of the Zoo there is a public foot-bridge over the canal that runs through Regent's Park. We soon came to realise that by climbing over the parapet and dropping down onto the towpath all we had to do was walk under the bridge, scramble up the bank, climb over a fence and we were in the Zoo! Many illicit hours were spent there on sunny days, watching the animals while eating our sandwiches and, if we could afford it, sharing a penny bottle of Tizer, 'The Appetizer'.

It was to be in Regent's Park that fate decreed I would perform my one and only act of heroism. I can't remember why Alice Rowe was with us that day. Girls were not encouraged to join our expeditions to the park because they slowed you down. They couldn't run fast, they couldn't climb trees, and they cried if they fell over. I can only think that Albie Rowe's mum had insisted he take her along. There were four of us that day: Me, my brother Charlie, Albie Rowe and his little sister, Alice. We were standing by the side of the children's boating pool watching the kids splashing about in their paddle boats, when Alice fell in.

The pond wasn't very deep, about two or three feet I suppose, but the water was much muddied and Alice quickly disappeared from sight. Although I couldn't swim (I still can't) I jumped in, groped frantically around in the murky water, and by sheer luck found her and dragged her out. A posh lady who had witnessed our little drama told me I was a brave boy, and gave me sixpence, which was a small fortune at the time. As we squelched our way home Alice became very distressed, so me and Albie took it in turns to give her a piggyback. When Albie's mum clapped eyes on me and Alice, wet through and bedraggled, she jumped to several wrong conclusions and, instead of the expected pat on the back, I got a clip round the ear. Albie got one too for good measure before she dragged them both into the house. Later, when she had heard the full story, Mrs Rowe came round to our house, apologised to my mum, patted me on the head and gave me a penny. My mum was very proud of what I had done, and although I affected to shrug it off, so was I. I wonder if Alice Rowe is still alive, and remembers that far-off summer's day in Regent's Park that so nearly ended in tragedy?

Our other big playground of course was the streets. It was amazing how inventive kids were in those days. Four old pram wheels and a plank of wood and we would knock up a serviceable go-cart. Two pieces of 4"x 1", three ring screws, a metal bolt and two ball-bearing wheels – and we had a scooter- of sorts. Newspaper condensed, moulded and bound with string would be a makeshift ball for a kick-about. Three chalk marks on a wall would be our cricket stumps. Hopscotches were chalked on pavements, ropes attached to lamp posts to make swings, and old bicycle wheels were hoops to run with. There were marbles (glarnies we called them) cigarette cards to collect and swop and, in September, conkers; which we would soak in vinegar or bake in the oven to make hard. There was no traffic to speak of, just the occasional horse and cart. So, again, we were in no danger. All kinds of weird and wonderful characters wandered the streets of my childhood: the muffin man, with a tray of fresh muffins balanced on his head, ringing a hand bell. the Wall's ice cream man on a tricycle with the slogan 'Stop me and buy one' on the front, the rag-and-bone man with a face straight out of a Hogarth print, barrel-organ grinders and knife-grinders. There was a newspaper seller called 'Flannel-foot' with a voice like a fog-horn that could be heard streets away. But there was one man whose visit was more eagerly awaited than any of the others: the 'jam-jar man'. He wore a long, ragged, rusty-black coat, a battered, wide-brimmed black hat, and a pair of black woollen mittens. He was tall and thin with a pallid, gaunt face dominated by a large, hooked nose on which a 'dew-drop' constantly trembled. He had no teeth and spat a great deal when he spoke, but he was welcomed with open arms and smiling faces by the children because of the wonderful contraption he brought with him. On the back of a horse-drawn open cart was a home-made, hand–cranked, miniature carousel; hand painted in startlingly vivid colours and inset with mosaics made from sea-shells, shards of pottery, pieces of coloured glass and pebbles. Music was provided by an ancient, wind-up gramophone with a large amplifying horn, and the 'price' of a ride was an empty one-pound jam-jar, or two half-pounders. Once the carousel was full (it held six children) he would place the needle on the record, start cranking, and round and around we would go to the tinny strains of Fucik's 'Entry of the Gladiators', though I didn't know that then, of course.

The ride only lasted as long as the record but what joy it was. Three minutes of bliss – for a jam-jar! When asked to name the modern invention he considered to have been of most benefit to mankind, Mahatma Gandhi is said to have replied, the sewing machine. I think my dear mother would have gone along with that. Her old, hand-operated Singer sewing machine was in constant use when we were young, as she struggled to clothe three rapidly growing boys on a woefully inadequate income. She would sit for hours taking in, letting out, taking up and letting down seams, hems, sleeves and trousers. Clothes bought at jumble sales or donated by charities were adapted to fit, and then passed down when they were outgrown. My poor mother always seemed to be sewing, patching, mending or darning. That's when she wasn't washing clothes, cooking, ironing and cleaning. The biggest problem though was footwear. Boots were expensive to buy and to have mended. Because we walked everywhere our boots wore out in a dismayingly short time, so my parents would try everything to keep them from deteriorating like covering the soles with steel studs called Blakey's, or using stick-on rubber soles, sadly with limited success.

Within three or four weeks they usually needed to go 'down the snobs' to be mended – if we could afford it. If not, pieces of cardboard cut to shape, were fitted inside the boots. A useful stop-gap measure when the weather was fine, but when it rained the cardboard would disintegrate which, in term time, would mean sitting in school with wet feet. During one spell of rainy weather I remember my elder brother Eddie had to wear a pair of my dad's boots and I had to wear Eddie's; both of them with newspaper stuffed into the toes to help them fit. Wellingtons were an alternative. I don't think they cost as much to buy as leather boots and their rubber soles lasted longer. We wore Wellingtons quite a lot; rain or shine. The other big problem of course, was food. Although we never went hungry, I can remember quite often wanting more. Our staple diet was bread, and each day we managed to get through three or four loaves. Potatoes were another mainstay, but whereas spuds were two pence a pound, a large loaf cost three pence. Which is why, every weekday morning before we went to school, my brother Eddie and I would do the 'bread run'. This entailed walking to Marylebone, which was about a mile away from where we lived.

In Marylebone, or 'Marrabun' as we called it, there were several bakers in the High Street who used to sell off yesterday's bread cheaply; and if you got there early enough you could buy three loaves for three pence. When we took them home my mother would wrap the loaves in damp clothes until needed, and then pop them in the oven for five minutes to crisp before slicing them up. Breakfast was usually toast and jam, and tea was invariably toast and dripping. In these cholesterol-conscious times dripping would be heavily frowned upon I suppose, but when the dripping melted into the hot toast and a pinch of salt was added, it was delicious.

The other source of cheap food was Seaton Street market. It is no longer there, but in the shops and on the stalls of that small street you could buy virtually everything at rock bottom prices. It also boasted three establishments that sold those three great working-class dishes: fish and chips, pie and mash, and pease pudding and faggots.

I must have been around eight years old I suppose when I first became aware of being on the receiving end of an ego-deflating expression my mother used, and was to continue to use, off and on, throughout my adolescent years.

In the mid 1930's short hair was *de rigueur* for working-class men and boys. But a 'short back and sides' at the barber's cost three pence for a boy and sixpence for a man; money my mother felt could be put to far better use. Consequently, somehow, she managed to acquire an old pair of hand-operated hair-clippers of the type barbers used around that time, and because my hair was judged to be the one most in need of a trim, I was to be the guinea pig for my mother's first foray into the hairdressing business. It was a disaster. I ended up with my hair a chequer-board of irregular patches of black and white; black where my hair was still attached to my head, and white where the skin of my scalp had been exposed. 'Mum' I wailed, 'I can't go out with my hair like this'. My mother's face took on a look of bemused disbelief. 'Who' she asked incredulously, 'is going to look at you?' The question was a rhetorical one of course, but at eight years old I wasn't to know that. I tried to make the point that if nobody had ever, even remotely, considered looking at me before; she had made absolutely certain that they would now! But my mother was having none of that. It had been intended as a put-down, and as far as she was concerned that was the end of it. It was my mother's way of keeping us kids firmly in our place should the deadly sin of vanity ever have the temerity to rear its primped and perfumed head.

To be fair to my mum, she really believed that what she was doing was in our best interests. We were in the middle of a deep and lasting Depression. Work was hard to find and easy to lose. The Labour Exchanges were full, the dole queues long. The way my mother saw it, rightly or wrongly, in the scramble for jobs it was going to be the lad who snatched off his cap and kept his lip buttoned who stood the better chance of being taken on. The cocky kid, who stood with his hands in his pockets with far too much to say for himself, would be destined to spend the best part of his teenage years standing on a street corner watching life passing him by. She knew only too well the humiliation and despair of trying to bring up a family without a regular, adequate income. It was small wonder then that she wanted something better for her children. 'A regular job', I can still remember how that phrase had an almost mystical resonance in the 1930's; because for most of the workforce it was to remain an unattainable goal until the end of the decade.

My uncle Harry had a regular job. He was a postman, and the envy of all his friends. To be envied for being a humble postman gives you some idea of the desperate search for security among the working classes of that period. It wasn't just the regular wage they coveted; it was the 'perks' that came with the job. A hard-wearing uniform and cap, with a warm topcoat for the winter months and an issue of two pairs of stout boots a year. But even better than that: holiday pay, sick pay, and a retirement pension. Not a very generous pension from what I can gather, but in those days any supplementary income in old age was a 'godsend', a favourite word of my mother's. I think it must have been in envy of Uncle Harry's happy lot that gave my mother the idea of getting me into the Post Office when I reached school-leaving age. At that time there were only two ways of procuring a job in H.M Post Office. (1) Having served in the regular armed forces with an exemplary record. (2) Starting off as a Telegram Boy. And that is how it came to pass that I found myself, a callow youth of barely fourteen summers, dragooned into service with the GPO. (Of which more later.)

To return to Seaton Street: There was a market there every day, but Saturday was the day the travelling market workers and the cheapjacks arrived, with their fancy waistcoats and strange accents. There was a man in a top hat who sold home-brewed medicines which he claimed could cure almost everything from alopecia to athlete's foot.

An old man with a startling facial resemblance to Punch who sold a bird-warbling device which you put on the roof of your mouth and blew through ("Amaze your friends!") but which never seemed to work. The old man himself made wonderful bird noises when he did it, but I suspect he could do that anyway, and that the 'bird warbler' was a catchpenny. Another man sold gramophone records, playing all the latest songs through loudspeakers, and when the Flat Racing season was over Prince Monolulu, the flamboyant racing tipster ("I gotta horse") would appear in his brightly coloured African robes and feathered headdress, selling lucky charms. But my favourite of the 'Saturday men' was the chap who sold confectionary off the back of an open lorry. He was short and squat with a hoarse, rasping voice and a squinty eye. Even more alarming was the fact that when he spoke he produced so much saliva that at times he appeared, quite literally, to be foaming at the mouth. Part of his sales pitch was to suddenly grab a handful of wrapped sweets and throw them into the crowd with the catch phrase 'suck 'em and see!' This is what we kids had been waiting for. Those sweets not intercepted in mid flight were quickly snatched up from the pavement seconds before one of his assistants in the crowd gave us a kick up the arse; a small price to pay, we felt, for perhaps half a dozen free sweets.

I loved Saturdays when I was a kid. For a start there was no school, which alone was cause for rejoicing. There was Seaton Street market, and our 'Saturday penny' pocket money from my dad. Whether he was working or not he never disappointed us, always finding us bright, shiny new pennies, and presenting them to us like gold medals. All these things helped to make Saturday a special day for me, but there was something else, something that transformed it from the mundane to the magical. It was going 'up' the Tolmer! The Tolmer cinema was a dilapidated building in the middle of the equally dilapidated Tolmer's Square, which was directly across the road from Seaton Street. It had once been a church and was damp, decaying, flea-infested and probably structurally unsafe; but to me it was a place of pilgrimage and devotion, and to be there at two o'clock on a Saturday afternoon was a joy that passeth all understanding. Two glorious hours of Tom Mix, Buck Jones and Ken Maynard. Of the Three Stooges, Laurel and Hardy, and Flash Gordon, all for three pence! Save up all week for that, we would.

Empty boxes would be begged (or stolen) from the market traders, chopped up into firewood and hawked from door to door for whatever we could get. It was very rarely that we missed out on what was, for us, the highlight of the week, more often than not because of the contribution made, albeit unknowingly, by Mr Budd. Like so many of the characters from my childhood, Mr Budd had the sort of face that would not have looked out of place under the eaves of a medieval church. He owned a rag and bone shop in Little Albany Street that was as dark and dank as a disused coal mine. But the thing that made him a hostage to fortune, as far as we were concerned, was his penchant for a glass or three at lunchtime in the pub round the corner, especially on a Saturday.

When he returned he would invariably fall asleep in a battered old armchair; it was then that we would strike. Albie Rowe and I took it in turns to do the dirty deed, which was to crawl into the shop on hands and knees holding a sack, stuff as many rags into it as we could from a big pile on the floor, and crawl back out again. All under the bulbous nose of Mr Budd locked tight and open-mouthed in the arms of Morpheus. The rest was easy; make a noise to awaken Mr Budd, then send my little brother in and sell his own rags back to him. Disgracefully perhaps, we never thought of it as stealing. It was getting our 'Tolmer money' and, with a bit of luck, a penny over to buy some sweets to share in the cinema.

Alan Patrick Herbert wrote:

> *Come to the pictures and have a good cry,*
> *For it's jolly old Saturday,*
> *Mad-as-a hatter-day,*
> *Nothing much matter-day, night.*

Except that for us it was afternoon, and we didn't cry. We laughed and shouted, cheered and booed ourselves hoarse in the conspiring darkness of our very own Picture Palace. However, as with most good things, there is usually a downside; mine was that the next day was Sunday – dreaded Sunday. It wasn't that you had to wear your best clothes all day (and woe betide you if you messed them up) or that all the shops and places of entertainment were shut, and that no ball games were allowed in Regent's Park. It made no difference to me. My Sundays were a complete washout anyway; and it was all my mum's fault. In response to a plea from the pulpit of our parish church for more altar boys, my mother, in a rush of religiosity, had nominated me!

Oh, what a falling out was there, and much weeping and gnashing of teeth, all to no avail. My mother had decided that a nod from me in the direction of piety would not go amiss. So every Sunday morning I would be there at the church; hair smarmed down with Vaseline, dressed in cassock and cotta, lighting the charcoal in the 'smoking handbag' – the altar boy's irreverent name for the censer. I served at four Masses in the morning, home for lunch, then back in church again at 4 o'clock for Benediction, which didn't leave much time for anything else. Even now, whenever I hear church bells going a feeling of melancholy comes over me. The only good thing about Sunday was that after tea we were allowed to play the gramophone. Ours was an ancient, wind-up model in a walnut cabinet with space underneath to store records. We had six: *Me and Jane in a Plane. Roll away Clouds. Red sails in the Sunset. Down on Jollity Farm. If I a talking*

Picture of You, and my favourite, a comedy song called *Ain't it grand to be bloomin' well Dead*. It was composed and sung on the record by a Variety artiste called Leslie Sarony, at that time one half of a successful double act called 'The Two Leslies'.

Curiously enough, many years later I was doing a film called 'The Pleasure Girls' and one of the scenes concerned a crooked card game in which an elderly man gets cheated out of his money. When I was introduced to the man playing that part - it was none other than Leslie Sarony! Over lunch I told him how much I had loved that long-ago record of his and asked him to remind me of the words. He did better than that; he sung it through for me, right there in the pub.

That dear old gramophone remained our only source of entertainment until, in 1937, we were given a wireless set. It was an Ecko; one of the early four-valve models with a separate speaker, and powered by a large, square 60 volt battery, a smaller flat one called a grid-bias, and an accumulator which had to be re-charged every four or five days. When it was switched on, an illuminated dial glowed with the names of exotic, far-away places: Hilversum. Oslo. Luxembourg. Allouis. Helsinki. Prague. Budapest. In actual fact the only 'foreign' station we ever managed to get was Luxembourg the commercial station, featuring The Ovaltinies, and a wonderful phoney American Western band called Carson Robinson and his Oxydol Pioneers; Oxydol being a popular washing powder at the time.

It was a wonderful gift but no one seems to recall who gave it to us. My mother couldn't remember and neither could my father, so we shall never know. But whoever it was and wherever it came from, it transformed our lives. Suddenly all the top dance bands of the day were playing in our living room, and all the great Variety artistes were entertaining us. There was Monday Night at Eight, Bandwagon, Music Hall, comedy, drama, sport and Children's Hour; a whole world of entertainment at the turn of knob. Miraculous!

CHAPTER 2

UNWILLINGLY TO SCHOOL

St Aloysius Catholic School for Boys was half a mile or more away from where we lived. There was a nearer school in Netley Street less than a hundred yards away, but it was C of E, a 'Proddy' school, so St. Aloysius it had to be.

It had been built in 1929, so although it wasn't Victorian in period, it certainly was as far as teaching methods and discipline were concerned.

The Infant School of the same name was in Phoenix Road, a few minutes' walk away, and it was there at the age of four that I was to begin what was to prove a painful, frustrating and ultimately futile journey through what was called the education system. Those early years were happy enough. I settled easily into the school routine and did well. The only teacher I can recall with any clarity was the one in my third year, Miss May. She was plump and motherly with a beautiful, serene face, and wore her hair coiled around her ears in the fashionable 'earphones' style. She was gentle, she was kind, she played the piano, and I adored her.

I can still remember her teaching us the song 'Golden Slumbers', and how sweet her singing voice was. It was a pity, in a perverse kind of way, that those early years were so idyllic; because it lulled me into a false sense of...well, not security perhaps, but expectation. There was nothing in those halcyon days to prepare me for what was in store up at 'big school' where, at the age of seven, I was dispatched. As I entered the gates of St Aloysius in Aldenham Street, my Via Dolorosa was about to begin.

The first big shock was being put into a class ruled over by a Miss Murray. It is difficult for me, even at this remove, to find anything remotely kind to say about Miss Murray. She obviously hated children and should never have been allowed to have anything to do with their tender, formative years. As I made my stumbling way through the different classes of St Aloysius I was to learn the hard way that each teacher had their own method of administering corporal punishment. Miss Murray's specialities were the boxing of ears, and the whacking on the open palm of the hand with a standard 12 inch wooden ruler. Not, I hasten to add, with the flat part of the ruler, but with the *edge*; an edge so sharp that, for a moment, it actually felt as though your fingertips had been sliced off.

She had also mastered the art – if that is the word – of boxing ears as well. The secret, as with most things in life, is in the timing. As the first blow to the side of the head rocks the unfortunate recipient's skull sideways, the second blow should be delivered immediately on the opposite side, preferably while the head is still moving; thereby ensuring maximum damage to the ear-drums and, with a bit of luck, causing minor concussion as well. Miss Murray was pretty good at ear-boxing. Mind you, she put in a lot of practice.

What I want to know is why didn't anyone warn us that the change was going to be so traumatic? I mean, one day there we were sitting at Miss May's feet singing Golden Slumbers, and the next being physically abused by a paedophobic harridan for talking in class! To show you how successful her teaching methods were, at infant school I had been a 'promising' pupil with consistently high marks; after one year with Miss Murray I was bottom of the class.

It is one of life's little ironies that when you think you've reached a point where things can't possibly get any worse, Fate tip-toes up behind you and whacks you over the head with a baseball bat. After an annus horribilis with Miss Murray, I was moved up to Mr Duffy's class. It was obvious from the start that Mr Duffy had taken a dislike to me, so at least I knew where I stood. It didn't make my life any easier, but when you start off with an expectation rating of zero, you are not going to be too disappointed if that is exactly what you get.

The year I spent in Duffy's class I learned virtually nothing. I spent most of my time trying to stay out of trouble to avoid giving him an excuse to cane me. I may be wrong but it seemed to me that I was caned, on average, every other day, sometimes deservedly, mostly not. There was only one thing from that year I remember with any pleasure, the school play.

Our class were putting on The Pied Piper of Hamlein, and although there must have been a dozen or more parts it seemed that I had been overlooked when it came to the casting. But fate was about to take a hand. One of the boys dropped out at the eleventh hour and, to my surprise, I was given the part. My dear mother hurriedly made my costume up for me. She sewed gold braid around an old chenille table cloth to make me a cloak, and put a feather in an old trilby of my father's for my hat.

On the night of the show during last minute preparations, a glamorous young woman suddenly appeared backstage (as it were) who turned out to be Mr Duffy's wife! I remember she was wearing a coat with a big fur collar, had short, dark hair set in the fashionable 'Marcel' wave, smelled sweetly of perfume, looked like Myrna Loy, and called old Duffy 'darling'. I had never heard anyone call anybody else 'darling' before, except in the cinema; and it came as quite a shock to me that my *bête noire* had a beautiful wife who must have loved him because she kept calling him 'darling' all the time. It transpired that she had come to help out with the costumes and was going around the cast checking everyone was properly dressed. When she got to me she crouched down, made a few minor adjustments to my cloak and hat, smiled, patted me on the cheek and said: "You'll do." Up until that moment there had been very little 'glamour' in my life – in fact none at all now I come to think about it. So this close encounter with a beautiful woman who looked like a film star had left me rather shaken – and not a little puzzled. What, I wondered, could such a lovely lady like that see in a turd like Mr Duffy?

Had I been made of less sterner stuff it might even have affected my performance, but I went out and played my part to perfection.

Not that the role was exactly demanding; indeed I only had one line. I was playing Fourth Townsperson and I had to say, "Clear out the rats or clear out yourselves, one of the two." An inauspicious introduction to the 'Theatre' perhaps but 'from small acorns...' It had been my first time on a stage and I had loved every moment of it. From then on I tried desperately to get into all or any of the forthcoming productions, but with no success.

Apparently my Fourth Townsperson had failed to impress, so that was to be the first and last time I was to tread the boards of St. Aloysius' Assembly Hall. However, a seed had been planted; a seed that twenty years hence would begin to germinate. At the end of that trouble-filled year we had the inevitable exam. I came 32nd out of a class of 34! I still have my school report for that year. In the space marked 'comments' Mr Duffy has written "His conduct leaves much to be hoped for."

Then it was goodbye Mr Duffy and hello Mr Green; a prospect that didn't exactly make my heart sing. For a start Greenie was an active member of The British Union of Fascists, and went on weekend marches through the East End of London, quite often returning to school on Monday morning in a foul mood and nursing a black eye.

He, like Mr Duffy, was short on teaching ability and long on discipline, and his favoured form of punishment was what he called his 'medicine bottle'. This was a flat piece of wood about two inches wide, half an inch thick and about 18 inches long with a handle at one end. One side was faced with leather because, at one time, it had been his razor strop. Now it was his bottom strop, which he applied to our backsides with diligence and, I suspect, a good deal of relish. The only good thing about being in Greenie's class, as far as I was concerned, was that he didn't seem to actually dislike me. I wasn't one of his favourites either, but that was fine with me. During my time in his class I did nothing to rock the boat, or to shake the branches of the tree of knowledge, and the year ended with me still anchored to the bottom of the class.

Then it happened - a change of fortune. I was moved up to Mr

Carroll's class. I was ten years old and my school life was about to take a turn for the better. There were only two teachers at St. Aloysius that had nicknames: "Nobby" Carroll and "Tapper" O'Sullivan, our headmaster. I soon came to realise that it was not out of impertinence they had been so dubbed, but affection. Mr O'Sullivan would have been in his mid to late fifties I suppose, but looked much older. He was a kindly man who liked nothing better than to come into class and take a lesson. He was always interesting, but if he thought our attention was wandering he would drum his fingers on the blackboard to re-engage us (hence his nickname). He had fought in the trenches during the Great War and would sometimes break off the lesson to regale us with wonderful stories of suffering, heroism and sacrifice from that appalling conflict. I saw quite a lot of Mr O'Sullivan when I was in Mr Duffy's class, mainly because I always seemed to be on detention, which entailed standing outside the headmaster's study after school.

Being the man he was, more often than not he would invite me in, sit me down and give me a short lecture on the importance of good behaviour, then give me the sandwiches he hadn't eaten at lunchtime. They were usually filled with a cheese spread called Velvita, which tasted like ambrosia to a hungry ten-year-old eager for his tea. As for Mr Carroll, being in his class was a revelation. For the first time in three barren years I was actually learning something, and I began to thrive. He gave me – all of us – encouragement and support and rarely, if ever, used the cane. Under his tutelage, at long last, I began to do well. So much so that in my first half-term exam I came 8th in a class of 32! Later on I actually won a scholarship to Brompton Oratory, the famous Catholic Public School in South Kensington. Which I was unable to take up because although the tuition would have been free there was the school uniform and some sports gear to buy and my parents couldn't afford it, so I didn't go. Many years later when I asked my mother about it she told me that at that time we were so poor, they couldn't even have afforded the bus fares to South Kensington!

It was round about this time that I fell in love with Valerie Piggott, and got knocked over by a car. The first event happened one evening after school. I was walking home with my cousin, Bertie Till, when a girl wearing a red coat came towards us. She had short, blonde bobbed hair, and a face of quite stunning beauty. As she passed by she gave me a smile so ravishing that it actually took my breath away. Maybe it was the onset of pre-pubescent precocity, a rising of the sap before the dropping of the testes? All I know is it stopped me dead in my tracks with small puffs of smoke coming out of my ears. Until that moment I hadn't really thought very much about girls, except in an off-hand, unchivalrous kind of way. Having said that, it behoves me to tell you that since the age of five, I had had a sort of understanding with Rita Herring, but that was different. Rita was Cyril Herring's sister and Cyril was my brother Eddie's best friend, and although we had both promised to marry each other when we grew up, in actual fact we were now just good friends.

But to return to the girl in the red coat. She had disappeared into a corner shop, so I waited outside. When she emerged a few minutes later she smiled at me again as she passed by, which had the same discombobulating effect.

Almost without thinking I followed her down the road and saw her enter a house in Cranleigh Street. I hung around outside for so long afterwards hoping to get another glimpse of her, that Bertie eventually got cheesed-off and went home in a huff. For the next two or three days I loitered near her house every evening after school hoping I might see her again, and eventually my impatience was rewarded when I saw her talking to some girls on the corner of the street. When she saw me, to my astonishment, she came over to talk to me. She told me her name was Valerie Piggott, that she was twelve years old and went to Exmouth Street School. How poised and self-assured she seemed, and how clumsy and tongue-tied I was in comparison. Before she left she told me that she was allowed out to play every evening from 4.30 to 5.30. "See you tomorrow then?" I said, with as much nonchalance as I could muster. "Alright," she said, smiled that bewitching smile, and went back to rejoin her friends. To say that I was smitten is a bit like saying Romeo was 'quite fond' of Juliet; I was absolutely besotted! For the next few weeks I wandered around 'like a tit in a trance' as Bertie Till so eloquently put it, neglecting my friends and abandoning Rita Herring.

My mother was convinced I was sickening for something because quite often I would skip my tea in order to spend more time with my beloved. Then one day she wasn't at the accustomed place. I waited a long time but she never came. Not the next day either, or the next. Fearing she might be ill I plucked up the courage to knock on her door. She opened the door herself, but only about six inches, and looked at me sadly through the narrow gap. "My dad says I'm not to play with you any more," she said, gave me a tiny wave and quietly closed the door. I thought about her constantly for a long time after that; still do occasionally. It's surprising how sharp the sting of rejection can be, even when you are only ten years old. As keenly felt in childhood as at any time in life, I'm sure.

When I was a schoolboy the 'luxury' of school dinners was still a distant gleam in the eyes of educationalists. All of which meant we had to go home for our midday meal. I can't remember exactly when the first pedestrian crossings appeared in London, but they hadn't been around very long, and had been introduced by a government minister named Hoare-Belisha. Marked with black and white stripes on the pole and with an orange coloured globe on the top they had immediately been dubbed 'Belisha Beacons'.

There was one at the junction of Barnby Street and Eversholt Street, which was then called Seymour Street, and I used it every day going to and from school. One afternoon, coming back from lunch, I reached the crossing and stopped. An L.M.S lorry pulled up on my right and the driver beckoned me to cross. As I ran across the road I was hit by a car coming from the opposite direction. I went under the car and was dragged along for about 20 feet or so before the driver managed to stop. I can remember lying in the road looking up at several faces anxiously looking down at me and thinking that one of them looked just like Mr O'Sullivan, before I lost consciousness. When I came to, I was being carried down the slope that led to the Casualty Department of the University College Hospital in Gower Street, cradled in the arms of a man, who I later learned, was the driver who had knocked me down. He was breathing heavily, partly from the effort of carrying me but more, I suspect, from the fear that I might die in his arms before he could get medical help. He kept muttering: "Don't worry, it's going to be all right," and every time he exhaled I could smell beer on his breathe.

The next thing I remember was my mother calling my name. When I opened my eyes she was sitting at the side of my bed holding my hand, her face pale and taut with anxiety. I hadn't been hallucinating. Mr O'Sullivan had indeed witnessed the accident on his way back to school from his lunch break and had immediately dispatched a boy with a note to my mother telling her what had happened and to which hospital I had been taken. Apparently, the driver had suggested taking me straight to University College himself rather than wait for an ambulance, and without more ado had laid me on the back seat of his car and driven off. In the confusion nobody had thought to take down his car licence number. Coupled with the fact that after delivering me to the Casualty Department he had left without leaving his name, this meant that he had covered his tracks rather successfully. I believe some attempts were made to trace him, but they came to nothing. They couldn't even find the driver of the L.M.S lorry who had beckoned for me to cross the road. Which was a great pity because having been knocked down on a pedestrian crossing by a driver who had almost certainly been drinking might have resulted in compensation of some kind which, in our family's dire financial straits at the time would have been a godsend, but it was not to be. I was kept in hospital for four days. I had been very lucky. When they washed off the blood and dirt they found I had a broken ankle, a dislocated elbow, lacerations and bruises all over my body, especially on my legs, and a dent in the side of my head. When I limped back to school about six weeks later I learned that on the day of my accident Mr O'Sullivan had assembled the whole school together, and led them in prayers for my recovery!

Up until now 1938 had not exactly been an annus mirabilis for me, but change was in the air. So was uncertainty. The threat of war was rumbling around Europe again like distant thunder, as 20 years after the 'war to end all wars', Germany was once more stoking the fires of global conflict. However, none of this meant very much to me at ten years of age. The summer holidays were coming up and me and my brother Charlie were going off to Brighton for a week, thanks to the C.H.F.. The Country Holiday Fund was a charitable organisation devoted to providing holidays for 'deprived children'. The holiday wasn't entirely free. Families had to make a small contribution to the cost. The total amount was eight shillings (40p) for each child, and you paid as much as you could afford into the 'fund' on a weekly basis for a year until you reached your target. C.H.F would then make up the rest. Somehow, my dear mother had scraped the money together from somewhere and, on the appointed day, we were picked up at the school and taken to Victoria Station.

For me and Charlie it was the first time we had ever been on a train, seen cows grazing in fields, fruit growing on trees – and best of all – been to the seaside. There was myself, Jimmy Martin, Michael Hayward, Frankie McBain and my brother Charlie all staying in the same house. I can remember clearly on our first morning in Brighton, walking down to the front and looking at the sea for the very first time and being overwhelmed by the enormity of it.

I can also remember the look of disbelief on the face of our landlady, Mrs Jasper, when she realised that there wasn't a pair of pyjamas or underpants among the five of us, and the only toothbrush belonged to Michael Hayward! Well, the C.H.F *was* for deprived children. What we did have were borrowed swimming trunks, in which we spent each sun-filled day on the beach. Mrs Jasper would give us all a packed lunch and a towel, and off we would go for the whole day.

With the salt wind in our faces and the hot sun on our backs we ran and jumped, hopped and skipped, cavorted and paddled; in your plimsolls, mind! Walking over Brighton's pebbled beach on sea-softened bare feet could be like walking on broken glass. When the sea was calm we would skim pebbles across the shimmering surface, seeing who could get the most 'hops'. When it was rough we stood at the water's edge shouting defiance at the incoming waves, then scampering back out of the way seconds before a big breaker dropped onto the beach with a roar, the sea water hissing and foaming among the pebbles before withdrawing for another onslaught; and we would laugh and cock-a-snook because we had outwitted the mighty sea. Oh, happy days. We returned to grimy London glowing with health and well-being, our bodies brown and faces freckled from the sun. Thank you C.H.F. wherever you are.

In the early hours of the 15th of November of that same year an event occurred that was to change our lives for the better. My sister Kathleen was born. This meant that there were now six of us living in two small rooms with no basic amenities. My parents applied to the Council to be re-housed – and we were. We were allocated a flat in a new block nearing completion in Queen's Crescent, NW5. It was called Montague Tibbles House and, in spite of the name, was for us a dream come true. There were three bedrooms, an internal lavatory and, joy of joys, a bathroom!

Of all the hardships suffered in my childhood the one I felt most keenly was the complete lack of any privacy, and the Friday night bath in front of the fire had always been a source of acute embarrassment to me. Now all that was soon to change so yes, 'a dream come true' is not too much of a cliché to describe the transformation that was about to take place in our domestic life.

One of life's sad ironies is the fact that it takes the threat of war to boost a stagnant economy and create jobs. The building of air-raid shelters had been given top priority by the government; public buildings were being fortified against air attack, cellars of houses converted into air-raid shelters, and so on; which meant that for the first time in years my father was in full employment, and that 1938 was the best Christmas we'd ever had. As well as the usual apple, orange and a bag of sweets stuffed down one of our socks Charlie and I were each given a soldier's outfit complete with helmet, breastplate and sword, while Eddie got the stamp album he had always wanted.

On Boxing Day we all went to see the film Treasure Island at the Regent cinema in King's Cross, starring Wallace Beery and Jackie Cooper, and that same evening actually went downstairs and socialised with the Bigsby family, something we had never done in the seven years we had lived there! The Christmas of 1938 was a memorable one for me quite another different reason. The Holy Rood Convent near London's Regent's Park, which is now a school, had played a large part in the lives of my brothers and me ever since we were infants. Having all, at one time or another, been taken to their free pre-school nursery, and later on, to the many outdoor children's parties they held in the grounds during the summer months. The Convent had been, quite literally, a godsend for impoverished families with young children, and, because of their good works locally, the nuns were loved and/or respected by everyone regardless of their religious persuasion.

This was just as well really, because every Christmas they would descend, en masse, on all the shops and businesses around Camden Town to cajole, or shame, them into donating food, clothing or money for the poor of the parish, of which in the 1930s, there was an abundance.

It was Christmas 1938, and the nuns of Holy Rood convent had prepared their annual Yuletide food parcels for the local old, infirm or needy, and had put out a call for volunteers to deliver them. Once again, my dear mother had immediately put my name forward. Actually, this time I didn't really mind. at the age of nine, going on 10, I quite liked the idea of being the bearer of gifts and glad tidings, and was happy to present myself at the convent on the day before Christmas Eve, and be given a bag with three parcels to deliver. Each of them contained, I think, a tin of soup, a small plum pudding, a packet of tea and two mince pies. Not exactly a Harrods hamper perhaps, but nevertheless most welcome.

By the time I had delivered the first two parcels it was beginning to get dark as I made my way to an address in Drummond Street, the home, if that is the word, of a deaf and dumb brother and sister. They must have been in their late thirties or early forties I guess and they were well known in the neighbourhood. Because of their grimy, dishevelled appearance and inability to comprehend or communicate (except with each other) the local kids, including me, always steered well clear of them whenever they ventured out onto the street. So it was with a certain amount of trepidation that I pushed open their unlocked front door and climbed the unlit stairs to the first floor where they lived, and knocked on the door.

Quickly realising they wouldn't have heard my knock, and not knowing what to expect, I gingerly opened the door and peered inside. What greeted me was a scene of such deprivation and despair that I stood for a moment wide-eyed and uncertain what to do next. The two people were sitting, huddled together, on the floor with a blanket over them, from where they regarded me with a mixture of suspicion and curiosity. There was no fire burning in the grate and the only source of light was a single candle on the mantelpiece. Still unsure how to proceed I held the parcel out to them, then put it on the table and stepped back. They looked at each other for a moment; then the woman slowly got to her feet, came over to the table and stood looking down at the parcel. In an effort to encourage her I pushed the package towards her, nodded my head and did a rather bad impression of someone eating.

To my great relief my clumsy efforts seemed to have reassured her, and she started to take off the wrapping paper and open the box. When she saw the contents she gave a strange wail, which brought her brother to the table, where they both stood picking up the items and looking at them in awed disbelief. My errand completed and, by now anxious to be gone, I turned to leave. As I did so the woman grasped my wrist, lifted it up to her face – and kissed the back of my hand!

Now, back in the 1930s, among the working classes, kissing was not encouraged. Mothers might kiss their babies of course, but once they started infant school it was usually a pat on the cheek for a girl and a pat on the head for a boy. As I made my way home to what, in relation to where I had just been, would be warmth and comfort, I was thinking about that hand kiss. Obviously the poor woman had thought I was the benefactor; and that troubled me somewhat. I felt I should have tried harder to explain that the gift was from the nuns of the Holy Rood Convent, but how? Perhaps I should have thought to take a pencil and paper with me so that I could have written it down – but would it have been understood? My impression was that in addition to the couple's already calamitous disabilities, neither of them could read nor write. Also, how at nine years old, do you say, in sign language, 'This isn't from me, it's from the Convent?' After I had related all this to my mother she told me not to worry, that I had been a good boy and had done my best. Then she, yes, patted me on the head.

CHAPTER 3

THE DRUMS OF WAR

In early 1939, as the day of our departure drew closer, I was riven with conflicting emotions. On the one hand I had the sense to realise that we were moving into a flat that offered a standard of comfort, privacy and hygiene we had never thought possible. On the other hand I had lived the whole of my short life in the same street. Moving away from the neighbourhood I had grown up in would mean leaving behind most of the things I knew and loved: the close proximity to Regent's Park, Seaton Street market, the Tolmer cinema, all my mates and Albie Rowe, my best friend. So it was with decidedly mixed feelings that I set out for school one morning in February from 93 Stanhope Street, and went home to tea at 57 Montague Tibbles House.

The new flat was everything our old abode had never been. All the rooms were bright and freshly painted, and the kitchen came equipped with a brand new electric stove and kettle, fitted cupboards and a big white sink with a direct hot water supply from a wall-mounted geyser. But for me the *piece de resistance* was the bathroom; it boasted a large white bath with shiny brass taps and a matching wash basin. And, lest we might be tempted to keep our coals in the bath as some working-class families were reputed to do, the Council had thoughtfully provided us with a built-in coal bunker! Because he was now almost 14 Eddie was to have a bedroom to himself, Kathleen's cot was in my parent's room, and Charlie and I were sharing a room – but (at last) in separate beds. I can remember on that first day going from room to room switching the lights on and off to reassure myself that at long last we really did have electric light. No more straining to read by flickering gaslight, no more carrying water upstairs in a bucket, no more sharing an outside lavatory with two other families and no more bugs, fleas or mice. No, this time we had struck lucky.

There were some drawbacks, all minor and mostly financial. The rent had rocketed to an astronomical sixteen shillings (80p) a week, more than twice the amount we had been paying before. St. Aloysius was no longer within walking distance, which meant catching the number 68 bus to school. And instead of the old penny-in-the-slot gas meter we now had a shilling-in-the-slot electricity meter; and with everything now on electric a shilling's worth didn't last very long. So although my father was working regularly – even putting in a bit of overtime occasionally – money was still tight. Even so we managed to buy a brown Rexine-covered sofa and armchair on the 'never-never', and acquired a new Bush electric wireless set in a black Bakelite case.

Although things were looking much brighter in the Malin household, out in the wider world the situation was bleak indeed. The threat of war was now a distinct possibility, and all the civilian population had been issued with gas masks as the unthinkable was fast becoming the unavoidable. As spring gave way to summer, and with the crisis deepening day by day, the government decided on the mass evacuation of schoolchildren from London. A tidal wave of cataclysmic proportions was about to engulf the world, and in my own minuscule part of that world I was soon to feel the first tremors of upheaval. I have often wondered what I would have done had I been in my parents' situation. Evacuation was not compulsory, but strongly recommended, because of the near certainty of air-raids on all the big cities. Having had children of my own I understand the dilemma they must have been in. In a time of immense uncertainty, and after much soul-searching, they did what they thought was best. Eddie had left school and started work, Kathleen was barely nine months old, so they were to stay in London with my parents. Charlie and I were to be evacuated. I pleaded with them not to send us away, but they had made up their minds and there was no going back. If I had had to make that same decision, in the same circumstances, I would have opted to keep the family together; either all go, or all stay.

Easy for me to say at this distance in time, but I still think it would have been the least disruptive and most compassionate solution. Three weeks later my tearful younger brother and I were standing disconsolately in line outside Euston Station, gas mask cases over our shoulders, home-made haversacks on our backs, and luggage labels in our buttonholes for identification. My mother had been too upset to come to the station to see us off, but then, just as we started to move into the station, my father appeared between two parked taxis and called our names. My spirits soared. Was it a last minute change of heart? An eleventh hour reprieve? In my imagination I heard him say: "I've come to take you home." What he actually said was: "Keep smiling," before we were shunted forward. By the time I managed to look back, he had gone.

Nobody had told us where we were going, so it became an excursion into the unknown. During the journey I had blinked back tears, swallowed my disappointment and tried to prepare myself for the uncertainty that lay ahead. Before we had left home my mother had taken me aside and gently explained to me that this was going to be a stern test of character as far as I was concerned. I was now responsible for the welfare and wellbeing of my little brother; and that I should always look after him and try to set him a good example. It was a burden I could have well done without at 11 years of age, but I promised to do my best. "Come on," she said as the tears began to sting my eyes, "you're a big boy now; be brave."

When the train finally pulled into Kettering station an hour and a half later, we still had no idea where we were. We were taken by coach to a small village called Rushton, about three miles away, and deposited at the village school, where a slightly apprehensive huddle of prospective fosterers were waiting to give us the once-over. There we were, Charlie and I, his hand tightly clenched in mine, waiting for a friendly face to take us to a new home amid the alien corn of rural

Northamptonshire. A Mrs Woolmer was to be that benefactress. She must have been in her early sixties I suppose, large of girth, ruddy of cheek and with a no-nonsense, down-to-earth manner. She lived with her husband Tom in a tiny two-up, one-down at number one Station Road. I realised that being uprooted from the bustle and clamour of London and set down in a sleepy village was going to take a bit of getting used to, but I was totally unprepared for what was awaiting us The plumbing and sanitation at 93 Stanhope Street had been early Victorian, but the arrangements at 1 Station Road were positively medieval.

Drinking water had to be drawn from a communal pump, and the lavatory was in a ramshackle, malodorous shed at the bottom of the garden. Inside, the facilities were just about as primitive as you could get; a piece of board with a hole in the middle, and a big bucket underneath, which was emptied once a week. No place for the squeamish or faint-hearted; especially in summer when it provided refuge to hordes of insects and lunch for squadrons of flies and where, in winter, an overlong visit was to invite hypothermia. There was no bathroom. In summer we washed in rainwater scooped from a large barrel outside the back door, in winter from the large black kettle that steamed and spluttered all day on the fire hob. The cooking was done on a huge coal-fired range which took up virtually the whole of one wall. Above the fireplace, suspended from the ceiling, hung a large wooden clothes-airer, festooned with underwear, socks, shirts and nightwear. So, not exactly all mod cons, but the house was warm and cosy and Mrs Woolmer was a wonderful cook – even baking her own bread. Mr Woolmer had been a gardener up at a big manor house until arthritis had forced him into retirement. He loved his garden and all its bounty, and still pottered around in it when he was able. I used to help him sometimes doing the 'bendin' for him. "Gardener who can't bend's 'bout as good as a clock wi' no 'ands," he said to me once. A true countryman, was old Tom Woolmer. Always had the same lunch every day: a piece of dry bread, a chunk of cheese and a raw onion, which he cut up and popped into his mouth with an old, bone-handled penknife; the same knife he used to prune and cut back in his garden! In spite of him being in his late sixties and barely able to walk he had remained, by some serendipitous oversight, the parish constable; his helmet, truncheon and whistle still hanging in readiness behind the back door. The Woolmers had two married children, Joe and May. Joe was a farmer, and played cricket for the village team. May lived in Corby and would cycle over to see her parents every Saturday lunchtime. On her very first visit she brought with her the Adventure boy's paper for me and the Wizard for Charlie, a cream cake each for our tea, and a quarter of boiled sweets to share, and continued so to do every week until the day we left. Thank you May, those small acts of kindness are still fondly remembered.

As for school, there was good news and bad news. The good news was that three of my school chums; Henry Hindes, Tommy Thaxter and Jimmy O'Donnell had been evacuated with me, and that Mr Carroll was our accompanying teacher. The bad news was that Miss Murray had come with him! Not such a daunting prospect for me as for Charlie – he was in her class! As it turned out, there was to be no return to the reign of terror she had instigated at St. Aloysius. Miss Murray still remained the thin-lipped, gimlet-eyed harridan of recent memory, but the feared wooden ruler remained in her desk drawer and ears stayed mercifully un-boxed. Maybe removing her from a grim London school and setting her down in a small, bright, cheerful village school had had a mellowing effect on the old bat. It could have been the benign influence of Mr Carroll, or she might even have felt sorry for us, who knows?

Being rather small, the village school was co-educational. Boys and girls had separate entrances and different playgrounds, but the classes were mixed which, after more than four years in an all boys' school, lit up my life like a shaft of sunlight penetrating a long-shuttered room. Of late, I had started to look at girls in a completely different way than I had done previously, and one girl in particular had caught my eye. Her name was Heather Flack. She was petite, had long blonde hair and blue eyes, and lived in Pipwell, a small village about a mile away. What I didn't know – indeed had no way of knowing – was that at eleven and a half years of age puberty was beginning to rear it's mischievous head. Sex education in schools was unknown, and my parents had told me nothing, so I was in total ignorance of the biological upheaval that was happening to me. All I knew was that it was all rather perplexing. I did my level best to ingratiate myself with little Miss Flack, but all to no avail. I even followed her home to Pipwell a couple of times, but it was not to be. Mind you, it must have cramped my style a bit having to drag my little brother around with me all the time, but in all honesty I don't think it made that much difference. I looked in vain for an encouraging sign, a kind word, an approving glance, perhaps even a smile – but promise came there none.

So, having been given the old heave-ho by a diminutive ten-year old blonde, I went to the other extreme and turned my attentions to the tallest girl in the school, a thirteen-year old brunette named Mary Goodman. It was doomed to failure of course. She was far too old, much too mature, and at least six inches taller than me. But she was sweet and kind (unlike the heartless Heather Flack) even allowing me to walk her home from school occasionally. One evening, after I had escorted her in tongue-tied adoration to her door, she suddenly leaned over and kissed me on the cheek. My fluttering heart had no sooner taken wing, when it fell to earth like a shot pheasant. As kindly as she could, Mary explained that it had been meant as a farewell kiss, and that perhaps it would be better if I didn't see her home any more. For the next few weeks disillusion hung heavily about me. Two rejections in such a short space of time had been a bitter pill to swallow. I did make half-hearted attempts to chat-up Mavis Clipstone and then Clara Binley, but when both approaches had been met with lofty disdain, I gave up.

My only consolation was that the summer holidays were starting and there would be other things to occupy my mind. With the 'soft haze of retrospect' all the summer days of one's childhood seem to have been wreathed in endless sunshine; however, the summer of 1939 was exceptionally fine. I climbed trees and rocks, roamed across fields, chopped wood for winter fires, went nutting and blackberrying and, when the shooting season began, was hired as a beater for three pence a day plus lunch, while the local gentry took their pleasure blasting birds out of the sky.

One Sunday in early autumn myself, Charlie and Henry Hindes had climbed onto a wall to get at some apples that were overhanging the street, when we saw Mr Carroll coming towards us. As we quickly scrambled down he approached us, his face heavy with concern. "I have something to tell you." he said. We hung our heads, expecting a telling off. "War has just been declared," he said gravely, then turned and walked away. It was September 3rd, my father's 39th birthday. A week later, early one Saturday morning, my brother and I were awakened by a great rumbling and clanking; accompanied by shouts and cries, and the shrill piping of a steam whistle.

We dashed to the window and saw a huge machine chugging and grinding its way up Station Road, billowing smoke. When it reached our house it turned and lurched into the yard of the farm opposite, where it swayed unsteadily for a moment before coming to a halt. It was my first sight of a threshing machine, and I thought it truly magnificent. On closer inspection it proved to be even more impressive. The thresher itself was almost as big as a double-decker bus, and was powered by a huge steam traction engine. Within an hour it was in full-throated, clattering action, manned by six farm labourers – and Charlie and me! We were probably more of a hindrance than a help, but we did our best, making up with vigour and enthusiasm what we lacked in expertise. The men on the ground pulled the musty sheaves from the stack with pitchforks and threw them up to the men on top of the thresher where they were fed into a large funnel which led to (I think) the separator. Those at the bottom dragged away the full sacks of grain or bound the straw up into bales. All day the air was full of dust, chaff, noise and laughter, and we loved every minute of it.

Towards the end of November our mother came to Rushton to see us. She had written to say she was coming, and by the time she arrived we were both in a state of high excitement. She had brought us our Christmas presents (not to be opened until Christmas morning!) and we were both overjoyed to see her. Sadly, her visit was to prove a mistake. We had been away from home for almost four months by then, and had settled reasonably well into our new life. Even the pain of separation had begun to recede. Now, with her arrival, the lid was lifted on bottled-up emotions, and when the time came for my mother to leave we were both pleading with her to take us back with her. By the time the bus arrived to take her to Kettering Station we were all in tears, and as it pulled away we were inconsolable. I remember Charlie and I cried ourselves to sleep that night.

The winter of 1939/40 turned out to be as severe as anyone could remember. Ice formed nightly on the *inside* of our bedroom window panes, and the soft soil of summer turned to stone under the petrifying frost.

"Ah, bitter chill it was!
The owl, for all his feathers, was a-cold;
The hare limp't trembling through the frozen grass,
And silent was the flock in woolly fold"

The unrelenting winter also took its toll on poor Mr Woolmer. His arthritis became so bad he was unable to climb the stairs to his bedroom and Mrs Woolmer was obliged to make up a bed for him every night on the sofa in the living room. For some unaccountable reason I cannot remember the Christmas of 1939; and I find that strange. Christmas, for a child, is a very special occasion and yet I can't recall it. I can't think why that should be. Perhaps it is symptomatic of the random selectiveness of memory, especially childhood memory, where sometimes trivial incidents can be recalled with pin-sharp clarity while important events remain shrouded in shadow. I don't remember my twelfth birthday either. What I do remember is the beginning of a sad decline in our relationship with Mrs Woolmer. She became increasingly exasperated with us for no apparent reason, constantly scolding us for the slightest mistake or simple misunderstanding, often accusing us of being ungrateful children, which wasn't true.

The winter seemed endless and spring long time a-coming, but come it did. Eventually. As the weather turned milder Mrs Woolmer started to send us out of the house. When we came home from school she would give us our tea, then tell us to go out to play and not come back until bedtime. At weekends we were only allowed in the house for our meals. As soon as we had eaten them we had to go out, whatever the weather. It was all very distressing and utterly bewildering because we had no idea what we had done to incur her displeasure. *Now* of course, I understand what the problem must have been. Mrs Woolmer was in her sixties and not in the best of health herself, and her husband had become a semi-invalid. On top of that she had the added responsibility of bringing up two young boys in a house that was far too small. It had all become too much for her and she just couldn't cope. Why she didn't seek help is hard to say. Perhaps she thought it would be an admission of failure, of not 'doing one's bit' in time of war. I don't know. It all came to a head one rainy Sunday afternoon. As soon as we had eaten our lunch Mrs Woolmer spoke the five words we had come to dread: "You can go out now." I tried to point out, as politely as I knew how, that it was pouring with rain, but she refused to listen and we were sent out.

Having nowhere to go we sought shelter under a railway bridge, where we stood huddled together both close to tears. After about ten minutes we saw Mr Carroll walking towards us under an umbrella, taking his after-lunch constitutional. Seeing us, he crossed over and asked us what we were doing out on such a miserable day. When we didn't answer he said: "Are you in some kind of trouble?"

When Charlie started to cry Mr Carroll asked me what the matter was; so I told him the whole sorry story. He listened in silence then said: "Come on, I'm going to take you back," and, despite our protestations, accompanied us back to the house. When we arrived he said to Mrs Woolmer something like: "I found these two under the railway bridge. Could I talk to you about it?" I could see Mrs Woolmer was flustered by the sudden turn of events, but she nodded agreement and we were sent up to our bedroom while the discussion took place.

I can remember the two of us standing apprehensively at the half-open door of our bedroom straining to hear what was being said. But the living room door was closed, the voices muffled and inaudible. After about fifteen minutes the door was opened and Mr Carroll called for us to come down. When we entered the room the atmosphere was strained. Mr Woolmer was staring out of the window, as though distancing himself from the proceedings, Mr Carroll was standing pensively, with his back to the fire and Mrs Woolmer was sitting at the table, face flushed, lips pursed. Mr Carroll spoke: "We're going to find you somewhere else to stay," he said.

Within three days we had been re-billeted. Our new home was to be the village rectory, a large Queen Anne house opposite the church standing in about half an acre of grounds, which on the face of it was a big change for the better. A house like that was bound to have indoor flush lavatories. There was a huge garden for us to play in. One of our schoolmates, Billy Lee, was already living there and a vicar and his wife were to be our guardians. On the appointed day when we said our goodbyes, Mrs Woolmer was close to tears. In spite of everything it had been our home for almost a year and, until recently, she had treated us with great kindness. So it was with regret, tempered with relief, that my little brother and I gathered up our few belongings and set off down the road to meet our new 'lady'.

Looking back, I suppose the fact that we had been given strict instructions to use the tradesmen's entrance should have rung a small warning bell somewhere, but it hadn't. We were met at the back door by Billy Lee and ushered in to meet the vicar's wife, who was waiting for us in the maid's parlour, a dark, cheerless, stone-flagged semi-basement, which was to be our living room. As we entered Mrs Horwood rose to her feet. She was small of stature, with a permanent look of disapproval on her florid face; a face which, I was soon to learn, turned to a vivid crimson when she was angry. In manner and bearing she was not unlike a Regimental Sergeant Major – even down to the small moustache – with all the charm, sensitivity and compassion those fine men are known to possess. Ten minutes after meeting Mrs Horwood I realised with a pang of dread that we had, quite literally, jumped out of the frying pan into the fire. Here was a veritable monster, and Charlie and I had been delivered into her clutches. The first thing she did was to issue us with a tin mug, a tin plate, knife, fork and spoon. This, she informed us, was our 'kit'. In the event of any loss or damage it would not be replaced. We were then given a verbal set of house rules and a written set of household duties. The house rules began by warning that we were never to enter the main part of the house without permission, unless in the course of our duties, in which case we must remove our boots. We should restrict ourselves at all times to the (cockroach infested) kitchen or our bedroom. We should use only the outside lavatory and adjoining wash room for our toilet and ablutions. We would take a chamber pot up to our room every night and empty it every morning in the sluice in the wash house. Our personal 'kit' would consist of a towel and face flannel, to be changed every fortnight. We were to be allowed one bath a week, all using the same bathwater, one after the other. The last occupant was to clean the bath before leaving. Some household chores were to be shared, e.g washing up, making our beds, peeling potatoes and exercising the two (spaniel) dogs morning and evening. The rest were delegated. Billy Lee seemed to have the cushiest jobs, polishing the wooden floors and furniture in the main part of the house. Because of his age (he was nine) and his less than robust health Charlie had been assigned lighter tasks: the cooking and cutting up of the offal to feed the dogs, feeding the chickens, collecting the eggs etc, which left all the heaviest, dirtiest work for me.

I was responsible for all the fires in the house, which entailed sawing up logs, filling all the coal-scuttles and replacing them in their rooms, cleaning out the grates and re-laying the fires with newspaper, wood and coal, and black-leading one fire surround each week on a rotation basis. I have to tell you that all this work had to be done *before we went to school*! However, this wasn't all. After school we were instructed to return immediately to the rectory and bend our backs once more in useful toil, usually in the garden. I had often wondered why Billy Lee never seemed to hang around with the rest of the kids after school, and now I knew. I learned later that we were doing the work formerly shared between a live-in cook/housekeeper, a maid and a gardener who, when presented with the opportunity to escape the virago of the vicarage by joining the armed forces, had all immediately volunteered and were gone within a month of War being declared. My brother and I were still in a state of shocked disbelief as we climbed the back stairs to be shown our bedroom, but worse was to come. It was a small attic room containing two canvas camp beds and one straw mattress on the floor. On each bed were three blankets and a pillow. There were no sheets, pillow cases or bedcovers. There was no carpet on the floor, no curtains at the window, and no electric light. When we went to bed we had to take an oil-lamp up with us. I can remember lying wide awake in the pitch darkness of that first night, in a room that smelt more like a stable than a bedroom, and being overcome with a feeling of utter hopelessness.

Before leaving us Mrs Horwood had advised us to get a good night's sleep. "We start bright and early tomorrow morning," she had warned. True to her word, at 5.30 am the following morning, ere the cock had shrilled his clarion to the dewy morn, she entered our room in her dressing gown carrying a lighted hurricane lamp, and a bucket of water for us to wash ourselves. Our first day of servitude had begun.

After all this time I still find it difficult to believe how *anyone*, let alone a vicar's wife, could treat vulnerable young children entrusted to their care in such an disgraceful manner. Did the Reverend Horwood, I wonder, preach love, compassion and charity from his pulpit every Sunday, knowing that none of these virtues were being put into practice in his own house? Perhaps he didn't know, although I doubt it; but *she* knew alright, and I will never forgive her.

To add to our misery she also proved to be the world's worst cook. Believe me when I tell you that Charlie and I had been brought up to eat virtually anything, but as hungry as we often were there were times when we simply could not eat the food she put in front of us. Big lumps of fat and gristle regularly appeared on our plates and once a week a revolting concoction called egg pie made from eggs preserved in isinglass was served up. Even the smell made us retch, and eating it was completely out of the question. We would secretly scoop it into some sheets of newspaper, take it out and throw it over the wall into an adjoining field, and scrump a few apples from the orchard on the way back to fill up on. Sometimes, before going to bed, we would steal pieces of bread and 'toast' them over the funnel of the oil lamp in our bedroom. We were usually so hungry that even the faint taste of paraffin didn't put us off. Now I come to think about it, that bedroom of ours would have been a death-trap in the event of a fire. It was right at the top of the house and the only access was by a narrow wooden staircase. Everything in the room was wood, canvas, cloth or straw; all highly inflammable! Then there was the lighted oil lamp we always placed in the middle of the floor while we undressed and got into bed. If that lamp had ever been knocked over...

> *"The swallows are making ready to fly,*
> *Wheeling out on a windy sky:*
> *Goodbye Summer, goodbye, goodbye"*

The summer of 1940 came and went, but we had little time to enjoy it. Most of our time was taken up with our daily chores, plus working in the garden and grounds, mowing the lawn, picking apples and pears and storing them away in cardboard boxes, sweeping up the fallen leaves etc. There was, however, one diversion that fine summer in which, to our surprise, we were allowed to take part. A Home Guard unit had been formed locally with men from the surrounding villages. They were mostly elderly and in various stages of decrepitude, but the *spirit* was there, and in time of war that is what really matters. They hadn't, as yet, been issued with uniforms or rifles; these were due to arrive shortly. In the meantime they wore armbands and paraded with pitchforks and shotguns. Talk of invasion was in the air and, if it came, our fearless fencibles would be ready for them; all they needed was a military exercise in which to hone their skills and test their readiness.

Because of the shortage of able bodied men it was decided to enlist the help of some of the local schoolboys to act as the 'enemy'. This was to prove their undoing. Twenty of us were recruited to represent a group of German paratroopers intent on sabotage. Mr Carroll was to be our 'commander' and we were given a biscuit tin with the word 'BOMB!' written on it. Our briefing was that we had been dropped to destroy any installations vital to the British war effort. When we pointed out that there weren't any, we were told to use our imagination. If we reached our objective, we were to place the 'bomb' there as proof that we had succeeded. The rules were simple. If someone shouted 'bang!' you were dead and had to retire from the fray. The following morning, in scenes that could have come from the George Formby film Get Cracking, we wiped the floor with them. We dropped down on them from trees, sprang out at them from behind bushes, laid doggo in haystacks until they had passed etc, etc. In no time at all we had knocked out half their platoon and 'blown up' a railway bridge. They may well have given Jerry a run for his money if put to the test, but up against a band of crafty, agile, inventive school kids, they were run ragged.

As winter began to bite, our troubles began to mount. In the absence of any kind of heating, our attic bedroom became bitterly cold at night. So much so that at times we went to bed fully clothed –

apart from our boots! As the temperature dropped lower and lower we finally plucked up the courage to ask Mrs Horwood for some hot-water bottles. What we were given were three house bricks and three sheets of strong brown paper! The bricks had to be warmed in the oven for at least an hour prior to retiring, and then wrapped in the brown paper. It was better than nothing I suppose, but not much; and stubbed toes became a painful nightly hazard. As the days grew colder my early morning duties became more demanding.

Then, as the festive season approached, the Horwoods invited four house guests to join them for Christmas, which meant I now had more fires to attend to every morning, and more coal scuttles to fill. The coal was stored in an out-building and sometimes, if there had been a hard frost overnight, I would have to use a pickaxe to break it up. I had no gloves, so by the time I had finished my work I was almost crying from the pain of 'hot ache' as I tried to thaw out my hands out in front of the fire. Why didn't I do something about it? Why didn't I tell somebody about our plight, or write to my parents?

Firstly, we had been brought up not to whinge when things got tough; if times were hard you gritted your teeth and got on with it. Secondly, the only person I could tell was Mr Carroll, who had been instrumental in moving us to the rectory, and would he have believed me? If he had become involved our situation might have been even more precarious than it already was. Thirdly, Mrs Horwood censored our mail. We were allowed to write one letter home each week, which she would read before sealing and stamping the envelope, and any incoming letters were opened by her before being passed on to us. However, a plan had begun to form in my mind. Whilst attending to the fire in the vicar's study one morning, I noticed that one of the drawers in his desk had been left open and inside were writing paper, envelopes, and a sheet of three-halfpenny stamps. A smuggled letter to my parents was now possible. I had the means, all I needed now was the incentive, some final affront to strengthen my resolve. When it came it was, in itself, no worse than many of the indignities that had been visited upon us; but it was to be the turning point.

It was Christmas day in the workhouse...Mrs Horwood had instructed us to set our table for lunch, then wait. When she was ready she would ring a bell to summon us to the dining room where we would present ourselves, holding a plate, and receive our Christmas dinner from their table. We waited quite some time before the bell rang, then we picked up our plates, knocked on the dining room door, and were bidden enter.

The scene I am about to describe took place almost 70 years ago, but it is as clear in my mind as if it had happened only yesterday. The dining room was warm and festive and smelt of cigars, with a big log fire crackling in the grate. The oak refectory table was set with fine china, silver cutlery and sparkling glass which was all laid out on an embroidered linen table cloth. There was a flower arrangement in the centre of the table and on either side silver candelabrum, each with three lighted candles. Sitting around the table were six people: the vicar, Mrs Horwood and two middle-aged couples.

As we entered, three scruffy, wide-eyed little waifs, holding our tin plates in front of us like begging bowls, the four guests regarded us with the awed curiosity of explorers who had stumbled across a hitherto unknown primitive tribe. "So, these are the little evacuees you're looking after, are they?" one man said, smiling affably. Mrs Horwood's mouth twisted into a grimace of a smile. "For our sins," she said.

It was at this moment that all the humiliation I had endured turned to resentment, and from resentment rapidly into rage. I had always known that there were well-off people and poor people, and that I belonged to the latter category, but because I had never really experienced social inequality at first hand I hadn't thought about it much – if at all. Now, suddenly I was acutely aware of the enormous chasm between our lives and their's. The stark contrast in our living conditions and their's, our quality of life compared to their's, and I became incensed by the injustice of it. But the final straw had really been Mrs Horwood's words: "For our sins."

When we returned to our stone-flagged, cockroach-infested living quarters I made some excuse and left the room. Knowing Mr Horwood would be entertaining his guests for a while, I dashed upstairs to his study and took from his desk drawer a sheet of writing paper, an envelope and one three-halfpenny stamp which I hid under my bed and bided my time. As soon as postal collections resumed after the holidays a long letter, written in pencil, was on its way to my parents telling them the whole sorry story.

I warned them not to write back, and begged them to come and take us away as soon as possible. On the first Sunday in the New Year, to our great surprise and unbounded joy, my father arrived – unannounced – and told Mrs Horwood he was taking us home. The old termagant was completely taken aback by the sudden turn of events and was, by turns, angry, reproachful and indignant, but there was nothing she could do. As we dashed gleefully up the narrow back stairs to gather our meagre belongings together, something must have been said between my father and Mrs Horwood, because when we came down he was standing *outside* the back door, grim faced.

I can still remember vividly, walking with my father and my brother down to the tradesmen's entrance of the vicarage for the very last time. As we passed the kitchen Mrs Horwood was standing by the window staring straight ahead; her arms were folded tightly across her breast, her chin drawn down into her neck and an expression on her crimson face which, if I read it correctly, was saying, 'This is the thanks I get!' Because our departure was so precipitate there was no time to make our farewells. I would have really liked to say goodbye to Mr Carroll (I never saw him again) to Mr and Mrs Woolmer, Billy Lee and my school chums.

In 1991, fifty years on, my brother and I drove back to Rushton on a nostalgic journey. We found the graves of Mr and Mrs Woolmer in the churchyard, and paid our respects. We looked once again upon the beautiful old rectory that held such unhappy memories for us, visited the village school, which was still in use, and wandered around the village. Nothing much had changed. There were a few new houses on the outskirts perhaps, but it still remained the quiet little backwater we remembered from our wartime childhood days.

CHAPTER 4

THE BLITZ –
AND THE AFTERMATH

When we got back to London in early 1941, St Aloysius, like many other schools, was closed so my parents were forced to look elsewhere for us to continue our, for want of a better word, education. Not having a great deal of choice the only seat of learning they could find was a 'Proddy' school in Grafton Road, near to where we lived. This presented several problems for me, not the least of them being that at almost 13 years old and big for my age I was still wearing short trousers!! Starting at a tough new school was going to be difficult enough without me turning up on my first day looking like an overgrown boy scout so I tentatively approached my mother with a view to getting me a pair of 'long-uns'. Her initial reaction was to say: "No. You'll grow up soon enough," but after getting the backing of my father and my brother Eddie she relented and promised to: "See what she could do." The upshot was a hand-me-down pair of my elder brother's grey flannels, and the promise of a new suit.

My 'new suit' turned out to be an unredeemed pledge my mother spotted hanging outside a pawnshop in Queen's Crescent market. It was a double-breasted, dark grey, chalk stripe, and was priced at fifteen shillings (75p). It didn't fit me all that well, but that didn't matter. What mattered was that I had a pair of long trousers in which to go to school, and a suit to wear on Sundays. Since returning to London Sundays had reverted back to the old routine of going to church. In the 18 months I had been away, going to mass had gone by the board with the nearest Catholic church being in Kettering. Now there was no excuse, St Dominic's was only five minutes walk away!

After the tranquillity and slow pace of a tiny village returning to London had come as quite a shock. The city had been under almost continuous nightly attack from the air, bomb damage was widespread and the people looked whey-faced and gaunt from anxiety and lack of sleep. After a brief lull, the air raids began to increase in intensity, which presented us with a problem: whether or not to continue going to the communal air raid shelter.

It was a decision Londoners had to make constantly during the Blitz. Thousands slept on the platforms of Underground Stations, others in Anderson shelters in their back gardens. Some took refuge in the space under the stairs, or crouched under their kitchen tables and hoped for the best. The surface shelter to which we had been assigned was cold, damp and airless. The bunks were as hard and unyielding as a slab of concrete, and there were only two foul-smelling lavatories for what was sometimes as many as thirty people. There was absolutely no privacy, and with young children crying and old men snoring all night, sleep was virtually impossible. A family conference was held at which we all had a say. The outcome was that we decided that in future, in the event of an air raid, we would stay put in our flat, all of us sleeping in our parent's bedroom, and take our chances together.

One night in late April there had been a particularly heavy raid, but at around 3am everything had gone quiet and we had all fallen asleep. Suddenly there came the most immense explosion and the next thing I remember we were all lying on the floor in pitch darkness, covered in glass and plaster. After we had reassured each other that we were alright my father told us not to move. He was afraid that part of our block may have collapsed, and that any movement might send the whole lot crashing down. So we lay there in the dusty dark holding hands, listening to the cries of the trapped and injured, the shouting of the rescuers and the clanging bells of the emergency services as they raced to the scene; until at last, at around 5am, the long-awaited dawn slowly inched its way up.

In the stark, early morning light we were able to assess the damage to our flat. Every door, window and ceiling had been blown out, down or off, and there was no electricity or water. We learned later that a land-mine had dropped on the other side of our flats, demolishing the whole block. Fourteen people had been killed, four of them children, and many more injured. Amazingly, no one in our family was injured in the blast. This was a miracle, attributed by my parents, to the picture of The Sacred Heart of Jesus that always hung on the wall above their bed, and which was still in place amidst all the debris and destruction. Further evidence, if evidence were needed, by my parents of Divine Intervention. I wasn't going to argue with that; when people are dropping bombs on you, you need all the help you can get.

We had indeed been very lucky. A woman who lived on the top floor above us said she had seen the land-mine, suspended from a parachute, drift low over the roof of our block, narrowly missing the chimney stack. That's how close it had been. Our flat was now inhabitable and we were officially classified as 'bombed out'. This meant we would have to be housed in temporary accommodation until emergency repairs were carried out. In view of the problems this would involve, coupled with the ever present threat of more air raids, my parents hastily decided on yet another evacuation; another upheaval in our lives. This time it was to include my mother and my two and a half year old sister, Kathleen. Within days we were all on a train heading north. After another journey into the unknown we eventually fetched up at Alfreton Station, from where we were taken on to the small, unlovely town of South Normanton in the mining area of north Derbyshire. We were hoping, forlornly as it turned out, that we might somehow all be able to stay together, but it was not to be.

We were split up, with my mother and Kathleen put up in one house, me in another, and Charlie, all on his own, in yet another. At least we were all living near to each other, but the separation was most keenly felt by Charlie. He was a sensitive little lad, never enjoying the best of health, and now he was all on his own without

Grandpa and Grandma Malin,
circa 1890.

Mum and Dad's wedding.
March 1923.

My Mum aged 16.
Isn't she beautiful?

Mum and Dad, 1923.

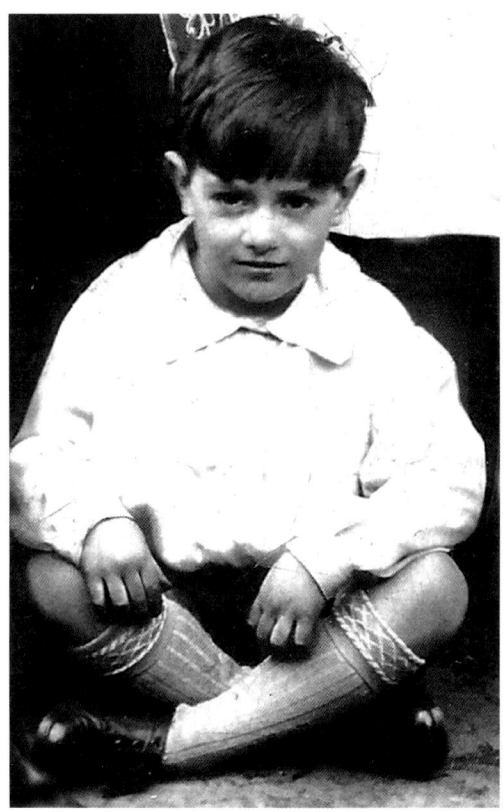

Me aged five or six.

Me aged three, holding the hand of my big brother Eddie.

Eddie in the Army, 1943.

From left, Dad, Charlie, Kathleen and me in 1949 or 1950.

*Friends in Dreamland in 1950. From left, me, Red-Hand Sid,
Rainbow Jack, Sid Lee, Long Harry, (unknown) Pip.*

George with Chrissie the monkey on his shoulder, Pip, Tod and me.

Me and Jack Mitchell out on the prowl.

Love's young dream. My marriage to Joan in 1953.
That suit cost £3.15 shillings!

My first passport photo.
I was 25 before I went abroad for the first time.

The photo, that landed me my first acting job at Swansea Rep.

Me with Joan and our son David in Ramsgate, 1964.
Sadly not quite the happy family we appear but we have
always remained close friends.

David as a young man. Like father like son?

Me at the feet of Judi Dench, – in more ways than one – in
'A Penny for a Song' at the Aldwych Theatre, 1963.

A happier moment in my relationship with Dorothy Squires around the white baby grand piano at her mansion in Bexley.
Second left is the wonderful singer Denis Lotus.

With the beautiful Nanette Newman in the film Séance on a Wet Afternoon, just after learning our only daughter had been abducted.

me to look out for him. He had been billeted with a Mrs Palethorpe, a widow with a young son who was almost as stern and unprepossessing as Mrs Horwood! My poor little brother had, once again in his short life, drawn the short straw. I, on the other hand, had struck lucky this time around. I had been taken in by a Mr and Mrs Ball, a miner and his wife. They were a lovely, middle-aged couple with three grown up children, and they treated me like a son. Their own son was in the RAF stationed abroad somewhere, their eldest daughter was married and the youngest, aged 17, still lived at home. Her name was May, she was dark haired, beautiful and voluptuous, with a wicked sense of humour and a delightful, mischievous personality, and in no time at all I had fallen madly in love with her. If only I had been that little bit older there might have been a glimmer of hope. An age difference of four years is nothing in later life, but at 13 and 17 the gap is unbridgeable.

May was sweet and kind to me, but it was a futile infatuation. At the age of 13 puberty now had me firmly in its thrall, and I was going through a turbulent, unsettling time. No one had told me what to expect and how to cope with it, and there was nobody I could turn to for advice except other boys of my own age, who were as much in the dark as I. South Normanton School was divided into two parts, boys in one girls in the other. Charlie and I had settled in as well as could be expected, when after a few weeks, trouble flared. In the playground one day I saw my little brother being beaten up by a bigger lad. Without stopping to think I went rushing over, dragged the boy off, and after a short, furious scrap knocked him to the ground and the fight was over. On our way home after school Charlie and I were approached by two boys. They explained to me that the lad I had duffed up in the playground happened to be the fifth best fighter in the school, and that I would now have to fight number four to establish where I stood in the pecking order. I had never considered myself a fighter, more often than not walking away from a confrontation, but this time it was different.

From the way those lads spoke I knew I couldn't back down. If I

<u>did</u> school life would become intolerable, not just for me but for Charlie as well, I had no alternative but to agree. It turned out to be a long, hard and painful slog. Each opponent they put up proving to be bigger and tougher than the one before, but I took them all on – and won! Three weeks, several bloody noses and a thick lip or two later, I was number one contender for 'Cock-of-the walk'. The reigning champion was a kid called Mosely, the boy I sat next to in class! He was a dark-haired, stockily built lad, with hard eyes and a knowing, insolent grin. Fortunately, he also happened to be a pragmatist as well. He had been quietly watching as I had fought my way up, and I think he realised that if the fight against me went ahead he would, quite literally, be on a hiding to nothing. If he won he would be no better off than he was now. If he lost he would forfeit not only his 'title', but a lot of playground cred as well. For my part, I was reluctant to take him on because I suspected that he would be a tough, awkward little bugger to fight. Also I had had several punishing fights recently, whereas he was fresh and fit.

One evening as I walked home from school on my own, Mosely fell in beside me and, after a bit of verbal fencing, we finally both, more or less, admitted that when you came right down to it we didn't really want to fight each other. This being the case we agreed to issue a joint statement to the effect that, as we were schoolmates and everything, we would share the title and consequently wouldn't be fighting each other after all; both of us quite happy with the status quo. Honour was served, face saved and respect retained, all without a blow being struck. It was my first lesson in the art of compromise.

I found living in a mining community a fascinating experience. I admired the attitude of the miners, their intense pride in their work, their prickly independence, strong family ties and firm friendships. Mr Ball was a gruff, kindly man. He was short of stature, broad shouldered, barrel-chested and his short, muscular arms were covered in blue-black scars, and when he was on early shift he would employ the services of a 'knocker-up'.

The knocker-up, usually a retired miner, would arrive in the early hours carrying a long wooden pole with a metal tip on the end, and tap on the window until he saw a light come on. At that time there were no pit- head baths, so Mr Ball would come home from work covered from head to foot in coal dust. As soon as he arrived he would take off all his working clothes out back in the wash-house, and stand there naked while his wife gently washed him down. Then he would put on some clean clothes and sit down to a meal of gargantuan proportions, always followed by the same 'afters' – a whole baking dish of rice pudding. He didn't drink or smoke, and his only interest was his garden, where he would spend most of his spare time. Mrs Ball was a plump, motherly woman with a rather sad, gentle face. She always made sure I had a clean shirt to wear every day, and gave me one shilling and sixpence (about 8p) a week pocket money, which meant that, if we walked there and back, I could go to the Odeon cinema in Alfreton on a Saturday afternoon and take Charlie with me. Best of all, she allowed me to use her son's bicycle, which became my pride and joy.

I had made friends with a boy called Fred Holmes who lived a few doors down from me, and on Sunday afternoons we would cycle over to the recreation ground to see if we could 'get off' with a couple of girls, without, it must be said, any conspicuous success.

The 'rec' was where the teenagers of the town congregated on Sunday afternoon for what was called, for reasons I never really understood, the 'monkey walk'. It was the age-old ritual dance of the mating game, where the boys strutted, swaggered and showed off, while the girls pretended not to notice, or feigned indifference. My big mistake was in pursuing the more mature girls of 15, 16 or even 17, a predilection that was to lead me down the stony path of rejection more than once. Because, of course, girls of that age weren't interested in a callow, spotty-faced youth like me. They had their sights set on far more attractive fellows, namely the ruddy-faced, crop-headed lad home on leave from the armed forces who, no matter how bovine of face or oafish of manner, simply by turning up at the 'rec' in uniform, would be guaranteed a gaggle of giggling girls, all vying for the dubious privilege of being seen on his khaki-clad arm.

In an attempt to level the playing field a bit, I devised a stunt which I thought might win me an admiring glance or two from the opposite sex.

Firstly, I had become quite adept at riding a bike with no hands; secondly, in a playground swap I had acquired a mouth-organ, which I learned to play quickly and rather well. So whenever I spotted a girl (or girls) that I wanted to impress, I would glide nonchalantly past playing something bright and catchy on my mouth-organ. I figured that the combination of trick cycle riding and musical accompaniment could be a winner. I figured wrong. The few girls who deigned to give me a glance, either raised their eyes heavenwards or sadly shook their heads...usually both! So having given it my best shot, and having had a couple of near misses with oncoming traffic, I decided to call it a day while I still had all my front teeth.

My mother had only been with us for about two months when she announced that she was going back to London.
Apparently the bomb damage to the flat had been repaired, and after eight weeks without my mother my father, like most working class men of his generation, was in dire straits. Throughout the whole of his married life he had never washed a pair of socks, ironed a shirt, made a bed, cooked himself a meal, pushed a pram or carried a shopping bag, and was now thrashing around like a drowning man about to go down for the third time. That's why my mother went back; why Charlie and I followed her six months later, I'm not so sure. Perhaps it was the advent of Christmas, the first one we would be spending all together since 1938. It could also have been that I was now approaching school-leaving age and my mother had plans for me in that direction.

When the day came I said my sad farewells to Mr and Mrs Ball, the adored May, and my beloved bike. It was in November 1941 that Charlie and I caught the train from Alfreton Station back to London.

In the summer of 1964 I happened to be in the Peak District of Derbyshire doing some location filming for a BBC TV series I was appearing in called Catch Hand. It was a Sunday, the filming had finished and I was driving back to London when I saw a sign for the turn-off to Alfreton and I decided to see if, by chance, Mr and Mrs Ball were still living at the same place. I parked outside the house and went round to the back door.

And there, bent over tending his beloved garden, was the unmistakable stocky figure of Mr Ball. He recognised me almost immediately and, declining his offer of a cup of tea in the house, I stood and chatted to him in the garden. He told me that his dear wife had died ten years previously, that May had long since married, and that he was now living alone, quite content to spend his twilight years in the same house he had lived in for most of his life.

Just before I left he said to me: "What's tha doin' wi' thasen these days?" I told him I was now an actor appearing regularly on TV. "Tha'll not be goin' down t'pit then?" he said with a twinkle.

CHAPTER 5

HEY, HO! HEY, HO!
IT'S OFF TO WORK WE GO

Do you remember when milkmen used to yodel? When I was a kid, as he put the bottles on your doorstep the 'milkie' would give a quick yo-do-lay-he-do. The reason I ask is that almost as soon as I was back in London I had got myself an early morning, part-time job as a milkman. Mr and Mrs Philips had a small dairy in Malden Road and, as he was getting on in years, Mr Phillips needed someone to help him out on his daily milk round, and yes, he used to yodel at the moment of delivery! The pay was ten shillings (50p) a week, and believe me when I tell you that never was ten bob more hard-earned. Especially since I only pocketed half a crown (12p) of it, the other seven shillings and sixpence (38p) going to my mother.

As I made my way to work at around 5.30 am on my first day it had begun to snow. But if conditions outside were wintry, inside the stone-flagged bottling shed at the rear of the shop the conditions were positively arctic! By the time we had loaded up the old-fashioned hand cart, my hands and feet were in the early stages of frostbite. As I trundled the top-heavy milk float round the back streets of Kentish Town I began to understand why Mr Phillips had taken me on. It was like trying to push a medium sized car with the handbrake on. Not only that, it was impossible (for me anyway) to control properly, having an alarming tendency to peel off to the left.

As soon as I met any rising ground I would do my Sisyphus impression, never quite making it to the top until Mr Phillips came to my aid. By the same token, any incline had me frantically leaning backwards at an angle of 45 degrees in an effort to prevent the float careering downhill out of control. Incidentally, why they were called 'floats' I'll never know; float was the one thing they *didn't* do!

This unique form of early morning torture was to continue for five long months until, eventually, I left school.

St Aloysius had reopened with a completely new staff, and it was there that I idled away the last, futile months of my schooldays. It was Easter 1942. I was 14 years old and could read, write, and do simple arithmetic. Not exactly the best qualifications with which to face the outside world, but then, little was expected of kids from my background. Ambition, especially the ideas-above–one's-station kind, was not encouraged. As it turned out, my fate had already been decided. I was to be a Post Office telegram boy. Brooking no argument, my mother had sent off for the job application form. In a short space of time I had been interviewed, medically examined, and accepted into the proud ranks of the GPO West Central Division; and how I hated it.

On my first day we were given a button-stick and a tin of Brasso and informed that buttons, cap-badge, belt buckle and boots were to be polished every morning, trousers to be pressed regularly, and caps to be worn at all times when on duty. The new recruits were then taken into an ante-room and given a short lecture, the object of which was to warn us of the danger of certain deviant men. Should anyone approach us and make an improper suggestion, or offer us money to accompany them somewhere, we were to refuse, notify the nearest policeman, and report the incident to our superiors on our return to base. I looked around at the new intake with their short haircuts, spotty faces and sticky-out ears, and wondered how on earth anyone could possibly find any of us the least bit interesting, sexually or otherwise. Perhaps sensing a certain incredulity on our part he added by way of explanation: "It's the uniform, you see." Mmm, hadn't thought about that.

The starting pay for a telegram boy at that time was a niggardly one pound a week which, after deductions, was reduced to eighteen shillings and nine pence, a beggarly sum even by the standards of the day. But if you wanted a secure, regular job in the Post Office you had to accept it. I didn't *want* a secure job in the Post Office but I had to accept it – for the nonce. As with all my dear mother's efforts on my behalf everything was always done with the best of intentions, and with my best interests at heart.

When I told her I didn't want to be a telegram boy, that I didn't want to be earning a pound a week when other boys of the same age were earning twenty-five or even thirty shillings, she said: "One day you will thank me." So for a while I soldiered on. During that first year only two events of any significance come to mind, both of which ended in disaster. There was a boy in our group named Hewitt who, for reasons I won't go into, was known as 'Tonker'. Suffice to say, Tonker was sixteen years old and seemed to spend an inordinate amount of time in the lavatory. On my way back to base one afternoon after delivering some telegrams Tonker fell in beside me and said he had something fantastic to show me. When I asked what it was he said, mysteriously: "Not here," and by a sideways nod of the head and a swivel of the eyes, indicated I was to follow him. We made our way to Bloomsbury Square, which was nearby, and sat down on a bench; whereupon he produced from inside his tunic a copy of the magazine Health and Efficiency.

For those of you too young or perhaps too innocent to know about this periodical, I have to tell you that it contained pictures of naked ladies. Incidentally, why it was called Health and Efficiency has always been a mystery to me. The women featured in its pages were young, usually blonde and always buxom. Indeed, some might even be described as 'strapping'. Breasts and buttocks of all shapes and sizes abounded on every page, but of genitalia there was none. Because, to conform to the moral climate and publishing restrictions of the day, all 'private parts' had been air-brushed out. Still eye-popping stuff though, especially to a priapic young fellow like me. As it began to dawn on me why he spent so much time in the lavatory, Tonker took me into his confidence and explained that he lent out the magazine to a small but select list of subscribers for the modest sum of a penny a day, and that he was prepared to include me among that elite. There was, however, one proviso: if the magazine was lost, stolen, or for any other reason not returned, the borrower would be liable to pay the full amount of a replacement. I gave Tonker tuppence for a two-day borrow, and stuffed the magazine inside my tunic.

That night I spent in my bedroom poring, goggle- eyed over its well-thumbed pages. It was indeed such stuff as wet-dreams are made on! The following morning I carefully concealed the magazine under some clothes at the bottom of one of my drawers before setting off for work. When I returned home that same night I realised something was wrong when I saw Charlie ducking into his room like a startled fawn. My mother came out of the kitchen and said coldly: "Your father wants to see you in the living room." Oddly enough I had no idea what the trouble could be – until I entered the room. My father was standing by the fireplace. In his hand was my borrowed copy of Health and Efficiency which he then held aloft. "What," he demanded to know, "is *this*?" I started to explain that it wasn't mine, and that it had been loaned to me by one of the boys at work, but my father interrupted me. "How dare you bring this filth in here?" he thundered. "This is a house of God." And so saying, threw the magazine onto the fire. It took me a long time to live that one down; and even longer to pay Tonker the shilling I owed him!

A few months later I saw a way of getting back into my father's good books. He had always been a big fan of boxing, my dad, getting up at 3am one morning in 1937 to listen to the Joe Louis v Tommy Farr world heavyweight title fight on the radio. Anyway, looking at the notice board at work one day I saw an appeal for boys to join the GPO Amateur Boxing Club. I made a few enquiries and discovered that one of the perks of being in the team was that you were allowed time off from work in order to train. Remembering how I had taken on all-comers at South Normanton School and fought my way up to top dog, I thought: "Why not?"

In training I did well enough for the instructor to put me down as 'above average'. Not the most enthusiastic of appraisals perhaps, but it was early days yet. I hadn't told my father what I was doing. I wanted to go on and win my first fight, show him my certificate, then sit back and bask in the warm glow of his admiration. Alas, as so often the case with best laid plans, mine were about to gang disastrously agley.

For a start, on the morning of my first bout I woke up with a slight cold. Secondly, and far more importantly, the boy I had been matched with – a novice like me – had withdrawn at the eleventh hour and had been substituted by a far more experienced lad named McSweeny. For those of a sensitive nature I will spare you the more lurid details of what followed. Suffice to say that McSweeny knocked six different kinds of shit out of me for three interminable rounds without me landing a glove on him. Afterwards everyone patted me on the back and said well done, but the consensus of opinion was that I should never have been in the same ring as McSweeny in the first place. (Why didn't someone say that *before* the fight?) You know, there comes a time in every pugilist's life when he realises the time has come for him to hang up his boxing gloves. I made that decision two minutes after the end of my first fight. The only fortunate thing in the whole sorry affair was that McSweeny didn't pack a really heavy punch. If he had, I might not have been going home on the 68 bus that night. I could have been on my way to the nearest hospital in an ambulance!

From then on my career prospects with the GPO went rapidly downhill. My cap-badge, buttons and belt buckle began to turn green from neglect, my uniform trousers remained un-pressed and (shock, horror!) my World War One short back and sides haircut, which was *de rigueur*, was abandoned. In short I wanted out. To hurry things along a bit I stopped delivering the telegrams entrusted to me. Instead of taking them to their destinations I stuffed them in the back of my pouch and went and played the pin-ball machines in a nearby cafe instead. It was now only a matter of time before I was apprehended, and sure enough within days I was nabbed by the GPO Investigation Department, hauled in front of the authorities, interrogated and suspended. A week later I was ordered to hand in my belt and pouch and drummed out of the service in disgrace. It had been touch and go whether I would face charges of 'wilfully obstructing the delivery of HM mail'. In the event I was let off with an admonition. To my mother's despair, I immediately got another job as a builder's labourer at twenty five shillings a week.

This was more like it, hard, dirty work. No more poncing about in a soppy uniform delivering telegrams. This was a man's job in a man's world, and for the first time since leaving school I was not ashamed to tell people what I did for a living.

It was round about this time that my father was called up into the army – again! My memory of exactly how this came about is a bit sketchy, but I seem to remember the government had begun conscripting older men for non-combatant duties in order to release younger recruits for active service. And that was how, at the age of 42, my father found himself enlisted into the Royal Army Medical Corps.

It now behoves me to tell you a little about my dad. I say 'a little' because I never really knew very much about my father. He was an intensely private man who, I suspect, never discussed his innermost thoughts and feelings with anybody, even my mother. I think one of the reasons for this was the fact that he found it difficult to express himself adequately. He was a modest, self-effacing man: a devout Catholic, decent, hard-working and generous to a fault. Imagine our astonishment then, not to say disbelief, when we were informed by letter that my father was being Court Marshalled for (a) wilfully disobeying an order, and (b) gross insubordination to a superior officer.

It couldn't be. Not my dad, surely? But it was. My dear father may have had his faults but he possessed a strong moral sense of right and wrong. To find himself down on his hands and knees scrubbing floors in a military hospital was humiliating enough, but the fact that it was a *Venereal Disease* Hospital deeply offended his religious principles. So that when, one day, the Matron – who held the honorary rank of Major –told him his work was unsatisfactory and would all have to be done again, he picked up his bucket of water, threw it across the ward and told her, in no uncertain terms, that if she didn't like it she knew what she could do! When asked at the end of his trial if he had anything to say before sentence was passed, my usually reticent and inarticulate father came up with a rather spirited and impassioned speech.

From what I have been able to piece together he addressed the court something like this. I am 42 years of age. I was in the army in 1918, so I know what military service is like. I have no objection to being called up again. In fact I welcomed the opportunity to do my bit for my country. But what I cannot accept is the job you have assigned to me. I know how to use a rifle. Give me a gun and ship me out to wherever the fighting is and I will do my duty to the best of my ability, but I cannot, and will not scrub floors in a Venereal Disease hospital, no matter what you do to me.

Whether the court was swayed by my father's oratory there is no way of knowing, but instead of the two year sentence demanded by the prosecution, he was given a more lenient six months detention in a military 'Glasshouse', which he served uncomplainingly and never spoke of again. When he had served his time he was discharged from the army as 'unsuitable for military service' and he returned to civilian life. I was proud of my dad for what he did. All his life he had endured the whips and scorns of a harsh, indifferent world with stoicism and resigned acceptance. But, humble man though he was, there was a limit to what he would tolerate, and when that limit was reached he stood by his principles and was prepared to accept the consequences.

It was round about this time that I renewed my friendship with my cousin, Jim Chance. We had been at St. Aloysius together but had lost touch during the war. We were almost exactly the same age, having been born within a month of each other, and had much in common, including the same sense of humour. Jim also shared my abiding passion for the cinema and we would sit for hours discussing the merits or otherwise of a film we had seen together. Unfortunately, neither of us was ever in sufficient funds to take in all the movies we so desperately wanted to see, so one night, longing to see a film at the Paramount cinema called 'Laura' with Dana Andrews, Clifton Webb and Jean Tierney, and being a bit short on the old doubloons (a doubloon was worth about two pistoles at that time!) Jim and I went round to the back of the cinema, found an exit door open, slipped into the cinema and saw the film for nothing; we had 'bunked in' to our first film.

Bunking in, or 'jibbing' as it was sometimes known, was the art of getting in to a cinema without paying, and from that day on we never paid to see a film. The simplest and most effective method was to set up an 'inside job'. This entailed a group of lads clubbing together to put up the money for one of the team to buy a ticket and enter the cinema. It was always timed, as were most of our incursions, to coincide with the end of a film or programme.

The lights would come up and lots of people would be milling around; entering or leaving the cinema, going to the lavatory, buying ice creams etc. During the general bustle the 'doorman' as he was called, would open a pre-arranged exit door, wedge something in the jamb to stop it self-closing, and return to his seat. Then, one by one, the rest of the gang would sidle into the auditorium, mingle with the crowd, find a seat and sit down and enjoy the film. The only drawback with this method was that the price of a seat had to be found beforehand, and if it was a West End cinema (which it quite often was) it could be fairly expensive for us.

As a result Jim and I devised our own methods of jibbing. We studied the layout of every cinema we entered, and collected discarded ticket stubs for future use. When we left a cinema we would always use a side or back exit and wedge a small glass marble in the upright bolt-shaft in the floor, thereby allowing the door to close but not to lock. (It was amazing how long these immobilised doors remained undiscovered)If, by the time we had arrived the film had already started, I would give Jim a leg up and he would remove the light bulb in the area behind the exit door. This way no sudden shaft of light would pierce the darkness of the auditorium when we opened the door, and give the game away.

That was how we managed to see every major film (some two or three times!) that was released between 1942 and 1946, and all it cost us was our bus fares. Oh, happy days. By 1943 Jim and I were both agreed that the only way we were ever going to meet and chat up girls was to learn how to dance, so we took ourselves off to Farr's School of Dancing, an establishment situated above a car showroom in Warren Street, where the charge was two shillings for a one half hour lesson.

Two shillings was a lot of money to us, but we considered it would be money well spent if it did the trick. What I hadn't bargained for was the attractiveness of the female teachers. I can't begin to tell you the agonies I went through during those lessons, desperately trying to concentrate the mind while holding a pretty young woman in my arms, her lithe, fragrant body pressed tightly against mine.

Much to our surprise, after four lessons Jim and I had both managed to master the basic steps of the waltz, foxtrot and quickstep well enough to trip the light fantastic without tripping over our own, or our partners, feet. It had come at a price, but now that we could dance the game was afoot – so to speak.

For our Saturday Night hop we had the choice of four venues:

(1) Farr's School of Dancing, Warren Street. Admission fee Two shillings and sixpence. Dancing to Victor Sylvester records.

(2)St. Pancras Town Hall, Euston Road. Admission fee Three shillings and sixpence. Dancing to Stan Clayton and his orchestra.

(3) The Paramount Ballroom, Tottenham Court Road. Admission fee Four shillings and six pence. Dancing to Ivor Kirchin and his band.

(4) The Hammersmith Palais. Admission fee five shillings and sixpence. Dancing to Ted Heath and his orchestra.

The venue we would all have dearly loved to attend was the Hammersmith Palais. Not only did Ted Heath have one of the best bands in the country, he also had the singers Paul Carpenter, Denis Lotis and Lita Rosa. But in the end, as always, it all came down to cost. Five shillings and sixpence was a lot of money to us at that time, and when you added on the bus fares and a (soft) drink or two, the evening could set you back a hefty seven shillings and sixpence – almost half my weekly allowance. So, for the next year or so, it was to be St. Pancras Town Hall. During that time two events occurred, both of which, once again, ended in disaster. The first concerned a girl named Rachel. She was a dark haired, rather strange looking girl who, I was reliably informed, was a 'dead cert'.

Forever on the lookout for my first sexual conquest, I made a beeline for her the next time she appeared; danced all night with her, laughed at her jokes, bought her endless soft drinks, and arranged to take her home after the last waltz. The first knock-back came when she told me she lived at Whitechapel. Whitechapel was down in east London, whereas I lived way up north, but I couldn't back out now that the chase was on. When we arrived at Whitechapel underground station it turned out that she lived another ten minute walk away! In for a penny, in for a pound, I thought as we made our way through the dark, cobbled East End streets. When we finally arrived in the vicinity of her home I immediately sought out a secluded shop doorway, where we were instantly locked into a heavy snogging session. Things were going swimmingly when suddenly a torch was shone in our faces. It was Rachel's father who had come looking for his wayward daughter brandishing a stout stick. Before I could take evasive action, heavy blows began raining down on my back and shoulders, and strange curses, in what sounded like Russian, were hurled after me as I made good my escape. It took me forever to locate Whitechapel station, only to find that the last train had long since departed. Having no money for a taxi there was nothing else for it but to walk – all the way to Chalk Farm – a distance of about four or five miles. As I began the long journey home an air-raid siren sounded. In no time at all several anti-aircraft guns opened up nearby, with an ear-shattering roar and I could hear shards of shrapnel dropping around me. Taking cover as best I could I slowly made my way homeward. When I finally staggered in at around three o'clock in the morning I found my mother sitting up waiting for me, tight-lipped with anger and anxiety. Where, she demanded to know, had I been until now? What had I been up to coming home at this unearthly hour? Didn't I realise how worried she had been?

When I eventually tumbled into my bed, exhausted, footsore and frustrated, I had learned two lessons. (1) Girls of reputed easy virtue had vigilant fathers. (2) Always ascertain *beforehand* where a girl lives before offering to take her home from the dance.

The other fiasco concerned a girl whose name I never discovered, or she mine. Just as well really, seeing how things turned out. She suddenly appeared at the dance one Saturday with a girl friend, and as soon as I clapped eyes on her it was lust at first sight. She had long auburn hair, the face of an angel, a heavenly body, and breasts like two cantaloupe melons. However, it soon became apparent that even getting to dance with her, let alone getting to know her, was going to be difficult. Upon arrival she had turned so many heads that it seemed every man in the place wanted to dance with her. Every time I plucked up the courage to ask her to dance someone would step in ahead of me; and for the next two Saturdays I didn't get a look in.

By the time the third Saturday had arrived I had developed a heavy cold, but I wasn't going to let that keep me away. So with puffy eyes and a red, blocked up nose I took myself off to the dance and positioned myself as close to the girl as I possibly could without actually sitting on her lap. Then at long last the chance came: "Would you like to dance?" I asked in a voice an octave higher than normal. She smiled, nodded graciously, and walked with me out onto the dance floor. Then she was in my arms and we were dancing a slow fox trot together. Heaven! Bliss!

As we glided round the floor we started chatting, she said something amusing and I laughed. Well, no, I didn't actually *laugh*, that was the trouble. I sort of snorted - *down my nose*! To my horror a snot-bubble appeared out of my left nostril, and before I could reach for my handkerchief the bubble burst. (In more ways than one) The girl was sweetness itself: "Oh dear," she said, "you *have* got a nasty cold."

'Mortified' doesn't even *begin* to describe how I felt, standing in the middle of a crowded dance floor wiping mucus from my upper lip in front of the girl of my dreams. Suicidal would be a better word. I escorted her back to her seat, mumbled an apology – and fled the building. I could never face her again after that, and never asked her to dance. After a while she stopped coming. I've often wondered what might have happened had things gone differently that night. Perhaps a great romance was nipped in the bud – all because of a snotty nose.

1943 was the year my brother Eddie was called up to do his National Service. When he returned home on embarkation leave four months later he was more serious and thoughtful than I had ever known him. On the night before he left he said to me: "When your time comes, do all you can to avoid going in the forces." When I asked him why, he said: "Because you won't be able to accept the discipline – and the senselessness of it all." Three weeks later he was on his way to the Far East where, for the next two and a half years, he fought with the 14th Army all through the Burma Campaign.

As for myself...life consisted of moving from one dead-end job to another, bunking in the cinema, hanging around Camden Town with layabouts and ne'er-do-wells, and trying, without success, to lose my virginity. By early 1944 I'd had enough of labouring and had begun to look for something easier, cleaner and better paid. Someone I knew worked in the tailoring trade and seemed to earn good money, so I decided to give it a whirl. My first job was as an under-presser for a firm in Wells Street that made ladies coats. (An under-presser is the one that presses out all the seams and darts in a garment before the lining is added) It wasn't a difficult job to master. All you really needed was a strong right arm because in those days all pressing in the tailoring trade was done by flame-heated, fourteen-pound irons. After a few months I had a strong right arm alright, as bulging with rock-hard muscle as any weight lifter. Trouble was, my left arm remained as normal, giving me a curious lop-sided look when I took my shirt off.

After about six months I moved on to a small workshop on the corner of Tottenham Street and Charlotte Street that made children's clothes. Whereas in my previous job all the machinists had been middle aged or elderly men, now they were all women: 14 of them, ranging in age from 18 to around 45. As I was the only male in the place, apart from an elderly man who worked down in the basement as a top-presser, I came in for a fair amount of ribaldry and sexual banter from the girls. I didn't mind at all. In fact I enjoyed it, and found working in an all-female environment for the first time a revelation. The biggest eye-opener was discovering that women, in a group, could be just as bawdy and sexually explicit in their conversation as men, often more so! As fate would have it, it was while I was working there that I had my third near-miss with death. As the war had finally begun to turn in our favour the nightly air-raids on London had virtually ceased. There was, however, a new threat - the VI, a rocket propelled flying bomb known as the Doodle-Bug. Packed with high explosives they would be launched from the French coast, timed to run out of fuel when over London, and then dive to the ground with devastating effect.

The only thing in our favour was the fact that they made a distinctive, loud roaring sound in flight, which meant that you could hear them coming when they were some way off and have time to take cover. Every time the air-raid warning sounded we would all troop down to the basement and sit there until the all-clear was sounded. This meant not only a loss of productivity but, as most of the girls were on piecework, a loss of wages as well. One day the owner of the factory, a Mr Beber, called us all together to outline a plan he had come up with to try to minimise the disruption to the working day. This was it. The building we were in had a flat roof that was accessible from inside. A warning bell, wired to the workroom, would be fixed on the roof. In the event of an air-raid someone would go up on the roof to watch and to listen. At the sound of an approaching Doodle-Bug the alarm bell would be pressed and the workforce would make their way down to the basement, leaving the person on the roof to join them as quickly as possible. Then when the danger had passed everyone would return to their work. Of course the person on the roof would have to be a man and, of necessity, young and agile...14 pairs of pleading female eyes turned in my direction. "It's worth another pound a week in your pay packet, son," said Mr Beber munificently. I have to say, it was the prospect of an extra oncer in my pocket rather than the admiration of the women that prompted me to accept. Nevertheless, I was hailed as a hero by one and all, an accolade I accepted with my customary false modesty.

The idea was a success. Productivity increased, and with it the women's wages. It suited me fine too. It got me away from the pressing table for a while, and gave me the opportunity to have a crafty fag, smoking not being allowed in the workroom. One late summer afternoon an air-raid warning was sounded, so I switched off the irons and made my way up to the roof. The day was warm and sunny, so I decided to do a spot of sunbathing. It was a decision that in all probability saved my life. I sat down with my back up against a small parapet, and lifted my face to the sun.

Suddenly there came a huge wooshing sound, followed instantly by a massive explosion, the force of which blew me from one side of the roof to the other. If I had been standing up I would have been blown right off the roof, but as I was lying down at the time I was saved by the parapet on the other side. For a moment or two there was an eerie silence, followed by absolute pandemonium. Shaken, dazed and in shock I stumbled down to ground level. When I reached the workshop everything was in chaos. Most of the ceiling had fallen in, the windows had been blown out, and the women were either numb with shock or in hysterics, but otherwise unhurt.

After a while, when things had calmed down a little we all began to appreciate how lucky we had been –especially me. The cause of the explosion, (and the reason I hadn't heard it coming) had been a V2, Hitler's latest secret weapon, which had dropped less than a hundred yards away behind the Tabernacle Temple in Tottenham Court Road. The V2 was the precursor of the intercontinental ballistic missile and travelled at something like 2000 miles an hour; which meant there was no defence against it! There was a rumour that two other V2s had already dropped on London but that the government, fearing panic and a possible mass exodus from the city, had withheld the information. Once again it seemed I had dodged the grim reaper; my only injury being a punctured eardrum. Did it all mean something? At the time I put it down to sheer luck, now I'm not so sure.

When I left the job a few months later the women presented me with a polished chrome cigarette case with my initials engraved on the front and each one of them gave me a hug and a kiss. I was very touched.

The reason for my departure was the offer of another job, something different, with a bit more money. My cousin, Dennis Weaver, worked for a small, film distributing company called Equity British Films in St. Anne's Court, a narrow passageway between Dean Street and Wardour Street in Soho. His co-worker there had left. Dennis told me about the vacancy and I had filled it. Our job was to pack the reels of film into boxes ready for despatch, and load them onto the van, reversing the process when the films were returned. It turned out to be a cushy little number. Dennis and I had our own room on the first floor, and as long as the work got done nobody bothered us.

After working in the rag trade it was a joy not having someone standing over you all the time. Directly across the narrow alleyway from our room a young prostitute plied her profession. She was small, dark haired and attractive – at least Dennis and I thought so. She also did a brisk trade, with a steady stream of punters knocking on her door. I have to tell you that things had still not improved in the leg-over stakes. In desperation I had tried taking some girls out two or three times, in an effort to prove I was not just after one thing. But I was, and they knew it, so I didn't get it. There was I, going on 17 and still hadn't broken my duck.

What was to be done? There were always prostitutes of course, our neighbour across the alley, to name but one. The going rate for the full Monty at that time was a pound, but a pound constituted almost a third of my week's wages so, sadly, it was out of the question. Or was it? After thinking it over for a while I came up with a great idea. What if...four like-minded lads got together every week and each put five shillings into a kitty? This would mean that, one by one, we could engage the services of a lady of the demimonde without having to stump up a pound all in one go. It would be sex on easy instalments, a sort of bonk now – pay later, brilliant, eh? Well, not exactly, there was a snag. Dennis and I had managed to recruit two other boys into the scheme, but there was one big stumbling-block. No one wanted to be the last man in, so to speak. To extend the cricketing analogy a little further, those players lower down the batting order were afraid that once the two opening batsmen had had a good knock, they might well go off the whole idea and declare the innings closed – with four balls still to go! So, unable to agree, the plan was shelved. Pity that. With a little more trust in each other we could have had a really good thing going there.

CHAPTER 6

TB OR NOT TB?
THAT IS THE QUESTION

VE day. 7th of May, 1945. After almost six years of 'blood, toil, tears and sweat' the War with Germany was finally over, and the people of London, along with millions of others, were delirious with joy and relief. They were out in the streets waving flags, cheering, laughing, crying, singing, dancing, hugging and kissing in a great out-pouring of long-pent-up emotions. A little over three months later, on August 15th, Japan surrendered, and our family was overjoyed. It meant that Eddie had survived the War, and would be coming back. Within a few months he was among the first to be demobilised and, to great excitement, was home in time for Christmas.

Seeing my brother for the first time in almost three years came as quite a shock. The handsome, bright-eyed young man I remembered had changed. His face was now gaunt and his skin sallow, and although he wasn't yet 21, he looked much older. His army record had been exemplary. He had served with courage and distinction, rising to the rank of Colour Sergeant, and we were all very proud of him. While he had been away Charlie and I had been sharing a room because Kathleen, now seven years old, needed a room of her own. Now that Eddie was back it was decided that he and I would share a room and Charlie would sleep on a put-u-up bed in the living room. Not an ideal arrangement for any of us, least of all Charlie, but it was the best we could come up with in the circumstances. A little discomfort didn't really matter. What mattered was that we had all survived the War and, for the first time in six years, were living together under the same roof as a family.

Like many soldiers returning from war, my brother rarely spoke about his experiences, and for quite some time afterwards suffered frightening nightmares of being back in the jungle, often waking me up shouting warnings and yelling out orders in his troubled sleep.

One bright Sunday morning in December, not long before Christmas, Eddie and I went for a walk in Regent's Park. It was a crisp, sunny day and we stopped for a while on one of the bridges that span the lake, looking down at the ducks on the water. After a moment Eddie took from his pocket a rifle bullet and held it up. "Do you know what this is?" he asked. "A bullet," I said. "My suicide bullet," he replied matter-of-factly, "the one that we all kept to use on ourselves if capture by the Japanese was inevitable; or if we had been wounded and had to be left behind. I carried this with me all through the Burma campaign," he said, looking at the bullet. And with that, let it fall from his fingers into the water below.

Sixty five years on I can still recall that moment, standing on a bridge in an English park on a sunny December day watching children feeding the ducks, and my brother, barely out of his teens, talking about the unimaginable horrors young men like him had to confront, fighting a jungle war on the other side of the world. As we walked home to a Sunday roast and Forces Favourites on the radio I asked him if he would really have shot himself rather than fall into the hands of the Japanese. "Probably not," he said, "there's always hope, isn't there?"

As my 18th birthday drew closer I was becoming more and more troubled at the thought of having to join the army. In my naivety I had assumed that once the war was over conscription would come to an end. How wrong can you be? It was to continue for another ten years! One morning as I picked up the morning post from the doormat, there was a letter addressed to me marked OHMS, and I knew it had to be the letter summoning me to my army medical examination. Uncertain what to do I put it in my pocket and went off to work. Later on, still undecided what to do next, I wrote, 'No longer at this address' across the front of the unopened envelope, and put it back into pillar box.

To my surprise nothing happened. As the weeks and months went by it became increasingly obvious that simply by returning their letter to them I had forestalled my call-up, at least for a while. As the summer of 1946 began to fade into autumn, my whole life was about to change in the most dramatic way imaginable.

As the months had gone by it had become obvious that my brother Eddie was unwell. He had been losing weight for some time, had developed a persistent cough and was constantly tired and listless. Eventually he was persuaded to see a doctor, who immediately referred him to a Doctor Back at his chest clinic in Camden Town. Doctor Back took a sputum sample, and sent Eddie for some X-rays. A few days later the results came through. My brother had pulmonary tuberculosis. The disease and deprivation he had endured for so long in the festering jungles of Burma had finally caught up with him. As a precaution everyone in our family was X-rayed and received a clean bill of health – all except me. My X-ray had revealed a 'shadow' on my left lung, the consequence of sharing a bedroom with my brother for over a year.

At that time contracting tuberculosis was, quite often, a death sentence. There was no known cure, no antibiotics to combat it (Streptomycin, although discovered in 1944, wasn't introduced until November 1947) and not much in the way of treatment either. Being a highly contagious disease, TB sufferers were isolated as soon as possible, not just from their family but also from the general public. Eddie was sent to a hospital for ex-servicemen in the country somewhere, and I ended up at the Archway Hospital in Highgate. The Archway had once been a workhouse, and in 1947 was almost as grim and forbidding as it must have been in Victorian times. For some reason, now forgotten, I was taken to the Archway in an ambulance. As it drove through the hospital gates on that bleak January morning

I remember thinking that, to all intents and purposes, my life was finished. In fact, in a sense, it was just about to begin.

The TB ward was on the top floor of the hospital and as I passed through its doors my heart sank. Most of the inmates were gaunt, elderly men in various stages of decomposition, some drifting wraith-like around the ward in grey, hospital-issue dressing gowns, others lying motionless on their beds staring at the ceiling. To me it was a place where all hope had long since faded, and I wasn't far wrong. It soon became apparent that it was a ward for the chronically ill, the final stopping-off place on the way to Highgate Cemetery.

The very first night I was there, the old man in the next bed to me died. I was awakened in the early hours by the bustle of nurses coming and going, lights being switched on and screens being pulled around. On my side of his bed a gap had inadvertently been left between the screens and the back wall and I could see the old man's face clearly as he lay waiting to be taken to the mortuary. His eyes were open, his jaw had dropped, and his toothless mouth had formed itself into the shape of an 'O', giving him a look of startled surprise, as if death had crept up on him unawares - and goosed him. Some time later, in a different place, I read a poem by Shelley which reminded me of that unknown old man, and the others like him on that hospital ward. Here is the last part of it:

"Alas I have nor hope nor health
Nor peace within nor calm around,
Nor that content surpassing wealth
The sage in meditation found
And walked with inward glory crowned.
I could lie down like a tired child,
And weep away the life of care
Which I have borne and yet must bear
Till death, like sleep, might steal on me."

A week after I went into hospital the police made their long-delayed early morning call at our flat. My mother explained the situation and they went away, promising further enquiries. A few weeks later I received a letter informing me that because of my illness I would no longer be required to serve in HM Armed Forces. After a couple of months two pieces of good news revived my sagging spirits. (1) My illness was not considered to be serious. (2) I would be going to a sanatorium as soon as a place became available. In those days a 'san' was where all TB patients wanted to be. Situated in open countryside, it was there that the best possible treatment available at that time could be obtained; with the added benefit of fresh air and a wholesome diet. There was also the psychological aspect. If you were sent to a sanatorium it meant that medical opinion had decided you had a better than average chance of recovery.

Meanwhile, back at Archway Hospital, one of my biggest problems was trying to get a good night's sleep. A hospital ward has never been the best place to spend a peaceful night, and ours was no exception; the snoring, the nightmares, the calling out for urine bottles, etc. It was during one of my many bouts of sleeplessness that I became friendly with one of the night nurses. After a while, if she saw I was awake she would bring me a cup of tea and sit by my bed, and we would chat quietly together. She was in her mid thirties I guess, small and slender, with big brown eyes, short dark hair and a gentle, winsome face.

Over the next two or three weeks I learned that she lived locally, was divorced with two small children, and lived with her mother who looked after the children when she was working. She only worked night shifts so that she would be home in time to take the children to school in the morning, be there when they came home, and to tuck them up in bed before going on duty. I told her something about myself, although at 19 years of age there wasn't much to tell. But we talked about my hopes for the future and so on. I remember she once asked me if I had a girlfriend, and seemed surprised when I said no. During another of our nocturnal conversations she suggested that if I had trouble sleeping in the ward, I should ask Sister if I could have my bed moved out onto the balcony. This did not normally happen until summertime, but as fresh air was considered beneficial, my request was granted. Whether the air rising up from Archway Road on one side and Highgate Hill on the other could be described as 'fresh' is debatable, but I was allowed to take up solitary residence on the veranda.

The view from my balcony was quite spectacular, especially at night. I would sit in my bed looking out over the lights of London wondering what my mates were up to, particularly on a Saturday night.

Finally, the long-awaited news that I was to be transferred to a sanatorium in Surrey came through. It would mean fewer visits from my family and friends of course; but that was a small price to pay for what was, to me, a beacon of hope.

The night before I was due to leave Archway my friend came on duty. As she was straightening my bed she said: "I've got a going-away present for you. I'll bring it to you later on." At some time around 3am, I was gently awakened by my friend standing at the side of my bed. She put her finger to her lips, and then to my astonishment, not to say incredulity, took off her uniform, laid it on the bottom of the bed, and climbed in beside me. And it was there, in the most unlikely of scenarios and the most improbable of storylines, that one of life's sweetest secrets was revealed to me. Fifteen minutes or so later she got up, put on her uniform, kissed me and left.

Next morning there was an envelope propped up on my bedside locker. Inside was a passport-sized photograph of my friend and an unsigned note which read: "Think of me sometimes. x". I kept that photograph for a long time afterwards, but with the passing of time somehow, somewhere, it got lost.

It has probably not escaped your notice that I haven't mentioned the *name* of my sweet benefactress. The omission, I'm afraid, is not out of a sense of chivalry, it is because I have forgotten. After all this time I can remember her face but, sadly, not her name.

"And the best and the worst of this is
That neither of us is to blame,
If you have forgotten my kisses
And I have forgotten your name."

King George V Sanatorium was built in 1921 in Hydestile near Godalming in Surrey, and was known as 'Teebeeland' by the patients. It was divided into eight blocks, A to H. These were set in pleasant, well-tended gardens in grounds of about two acres, and surrounded by a six foot high wire-mesh fence. All the blocks were identical in design. As you entered, the lavatories, bath and shower rooms were on the left, patient's lockers on the right, then a long corridor with one single and two double rooms on either side, leading on to a circular dormitory at the end which contained six beds. On arrival I was assigned to G Block, and took up residence in the six-bed ward.

After the gloom, doom and despair of Archway, King George's was, quite literally, a breath of fresh air. The blocks were bright and cheerful, and staffed by jolly, motivated nurses. I soon found out, however, that there was one rather large fly in this otherwise soothing ointment. His name was Doctor Watt, a man to whom the adjective 'dour' didn't even begin to do justice. Because his post was an administrative one I have no idea what he was like as a doctor, but as a human being there was definitely room for improvement. He was a tall, thin lugubrious Scotsman, in his early sixties, who spoke very slowly and deliberately in a deep, sepulchral monotone.

His grim, forbidding demeanour suggesting that life was something to be endured – not enjoyed, especially in a sanatorium; which meant that King George's was run more like a prisoner-of war camp than a hospital.

The rules were:

(1) *Never* to touch, or make suggestive or ribald remarks to nurses or female ancillary staff.

(2) To strictly observe the 'rest period' (2pm to 4pm).

(3) *Never* to leave the grounds of the sanatorium.
(4) No fraternisation after lights out (9pm)
5) No alcohol of any kind.

You will not be surprised to learn that our commandant was known among the inmates (and I suspect many of the staff) as Doctor Killjoy. A man who, I was reliably informed, was in the habit of sitting at the window of his office on the top floor of the administration block with a pair of binoculars, scanning the hospital and grounds for any sign of disobedience or insubordination. All we needed to complete the picture were a couple of watchtowers!

At various times during my confinement at King George's I, along with others of a like-mind, tried to get permission to:
(a) Publish a weekly newsletter.
(b) Initiate a record request programme on the internal radio link.
(c) Form a drama group.
(d) Arrange for a weekly film show in the assembly hall.

All of which were vetoed by Doctor No. The one contribution I *was* able to make during my stay was to re-organise the library. When I took over it was in a sad state of musty neglect. Six months later I had catalogued and classified all the books, and re-instated the long-abandoned trolley service for patients confined to bed. It was, in a way, a repaid debt, because it was there on those dusty shelves that I discovered the authors, poets and playwrights that were to alter my life.

In those distant days before the advent of effective antibiotics the one thing all TB patients had in abundance was 'time'. Recovery was painfully slow and wearisome and treatments fairly basic. They consisted of bed rest which meant simply, rest and fresh air. Then there was the artificial pneumo-thorax and pneumo-peritoneum, which was a temporary collapse of the lung brought about by the injection of air between the chest-wall and the lung. Finally there was the thora-caplacity, a last resort operation in which the four top ribs were removed, causing a permanent collapse of the lung, and a concavity in the chest below the collar bone. I was lucky. In my case it was decided that bed-rest was all that was necessary. This meant being allowed up initially for one hour a day, then two, and so on until I was UAD, up all day.

The axiom about disease being no respecter of persons was certainly borne out at the sanatorium. Of the 16 men on G block alone we had a clarinettist from the BBC Symphony Orchestra, an ex-professional boxer, a bank manager and an English teacher. One morning I stopped to chat to the teacher. He had one of the prized single rooms, and was sitting on his bed doing The Times crossword puzzle. It was a chance meeting that was to bring about a sea-change in my life. After chatting for a while, out of curiosity, I picked up the almost completed crossword he had been working on. Even after he had carefully explained to me how cryptic crosswords work, and shown me how he had solved the clues, I was still completely in the dark. "Why don't you try one yourself?" he said. "Start off doing the simple ones and see how you go. All you need is a good dictionary, intelligence, and a fair bit of general knowledge; particularly of literature."

When I explained to him that my knowledge of literature was confined to the 'William' books by Richmal Crompton, and learning the poem Nicholas Nye by Walter De La Mare off by heart, he was immediately supportive. "Well, let's do something about that," he said. "Use your time here to good effect. There's an almost complete set of Dickens in the library; start with him. If there's anything you don't understand, ask me and I'll explain it to you. Any words that you don't know or are unsure about, look them up. You can borrow my dictionary any time you want." During my long convalescence I was to read most of Dickens, the complete works of Shakespeare, Trollope, Forster, the Brontes, Greene, Waugh etc, all prompted and encouraged by my mentor. I developed a passion for poetry and sent off for a recently published volume entitled Poetry of the English Speaking World, compiled by Richard Aldington. It cost two pounds ten shillings which was a small fortune, but money I considered well spent. In my opinion it is one of the best and most comprehensive anthologies I have ever read. I also became a dab hand at crosswords, an addiction that still has me hooked to this day.

By another of those strange quirks of memory, I am unable to remember the name of the man to whom I owe so much. I think his surname was Hunt, but that is only a guess. He left King George's about six months before my own departure, leaving me his dictionary and Thesaurus, and the rest of his books to the library.

Towards the end of 1947 I received a letter from my mother telling me that my brother Eddie had been moved to Archway Hospital. This was not good news. -Archway was the end of the line, and being transferred there from another hospital was a bad sign. Three months later another letter arrived telling me that Eddie was 'coming home'. This could mean only one thing. There was nothing more they could do for him. A few weeks later I was on post delivery duty and had gone down to the mail room to collect the letters for G and H blocks. As I picked up the pile of mail I saw in amongst them a black-bordered envelope, and I knew without looking that it was for me. I put the letter in my pocket, delivered the rest of the mail, then took myself off to a remote corner of the grounds where, on fine days, I could sit and read without being disturbed and, with a heavy heart, opened my letter. At the age of 23 my brother Eddie had died of advanced pulmonary tuberculosis. The funeral service had been held at St. Dominic's Priory, and the burial at Finchley Cemetery.

It seemed a bitter irony that after surviving almost three years of jungle warfare unscathed he had succumbed to a disease almost certainly contracted as a result of the deprivations he had suffered during his time in the tropics. I sat for a long time coming to tearful terms with our untimely loss, but out of sorrow came resolve. I became determined to make something of my life; if only for my brother who hadn't lived long enough to even spread his wings, let alone take flight. I knew the only way I could achieve this was by study; to observe, listen and read.

Every night I would lie in bed with my earphones on listening to symphony concerts, operas, plays, talks and quizzes etc; absorbing, discussing and retaining.

After much string-pulling I managed to procure one of the much sought-after single rooms. I told myself that this was solely for the purposes of uninterrupted study, but to be honest there was an ulterior motive, albeit a fanciful one. I had realised very early on that if there was ever going to be a repeat performance of the 'balcony scene' at Archway Hospital, it was never going to happen in a room with other people. Incidentally, at that time it was a seriously held belief that TB increased the male libido. (I have to say that I wasn't the best person on which to test this theory because, from the age of thirteen, *my* libido had consistently been at gale-force eight on the Beaufort scale!) It was for this reason, I was reliably informed, that most of the nurses at King George's were – not to be too ungallant – less attractive. This was a deliberate policy, so the story went, to minimise the yearnings of the long-term male patients. All I can say is if that *was* the intention, then it definitely didn't work, not for me anyway. Quite frankly, after over a year of enforced celibacy if an Old Mother Riley look-alike had fluttered her eyelashes at me it would have been touch and go, let alone wholesome, apple-cheeked, ample-bosomed, nurses! Sunday was visiting day at King George's, and all the 'up' patients would – weather permitting – immediately take their wives or sweethearts for a walk in the hospital grounds in an attempt to find a shady nook for a spot of alfresco nookie. Unfortunately, all the other inmates had the same idea, and in no time at all the whole area was as crowded as Battersea Park on a sunny, bank holiday afternoon.

One morning on my way to the library I heard someone playing the piano in the assembly hall. When I looked inside I saw a chap from H block that I knew slightly. We had shared a table in the dining hall a couple of times, during which I had learned that before contracting TB he had been a trumpet player with several dance bands. Now, realising that he could never go back to trumpet playing, he had decided to learn the piano, so that when he returned to the outside world again he would have some means of earning a living. Much to his surprise, when he had approached Doctor Killjoy on the matter the old curmudgeon had raised no objection, and had entrusted him with the keys to both the hall and the piano.

When I told him I'd always wanted to play the piano he immediately offered to loan me a chord book for beginners. It was a system showing part of the piano keyboard with dots indicating where to put your fingers, with the chord symbol written underneath. Over the next six months he taught me simple harmony and the rudiments of music, which set me on the road to learning to play the piano, something that has given me much enjoyment over the years and has, at times, been quite useful in that I could always pick up a pound or two playing in a pub when money was short.

I was finally discharged from King George's at the beginning of January 1949, a few weeks before my 21st birthday. Having looked forward to my release for so long, when the time came to say goodbye I was beset by conflicting emotions. Through my work in the library I had become a popular figure with many of the inmates, and although glad for me, they were sorry to see me go. In many ways I was just as sad to be leaving. For the first time in my life I had achieved something, made something of myself, and I was reluctant to let it go. I'd been a big fish in a very small pond but it had given me the one thing I had always lacked – self-confidence.

As a gesture of gratitude I left all my books to the library, even my treasured anthology; writing something pretentious inside the cover of each of them before putting them up on the shelves.

CHAPTER 7

ALL THE FUN OF THE FAIR

Several shocks were awaiting me back in the outside world. The first one hit me as soon as I stepped off the train. After almost two years in the cloistered calm and antiseptic cleanliness of a rural sanatorium, Waterloo station, with its dirt, dust, smell and clamour, was like a peep into hell. As I stood waiting for the number 68 bus amidst the bustle and roar of Waterloo Road, I had to keep reassuring myself that I had been born and bred in London, and would soon get used to city life again. The second shock was returning to our flat in Montague Tibbles House.

Everything seemed so much smaller and darker than I remembered and having to share a room with my brother Charlie, nice lad though he was, didn't exactly fill my heart with joy either. I soon came to realise how institutionalised I had become, how accustomed to an ordered, routine-dominated life; and suspected that getting back into the 'real world' was going to be an uphill struggle for a while. I was also concerned about what I was going to do, having no skills and no trade.

On my 21st birthday my mother gave me a gold 'keeper' ring that had (I think) belonged to her mother, and arranged a small party to celebrate my coming of age and my discharge from hospital. After a few weeks at home I was becoming increasingly restless, and found settling down much more difficult than I had anticipated. I started to go for long walks across Regent's Park on my own, trying to work out what to do with my life. As summer approached that problem was solved – in the short term – when I bumped into my cousin Dennis Weaver in Camden High Street. During my time at King George's I'd met a chap who had worked several summer seasons at Dreamland

Park, a fairground in Margate. He had regaled me with stories of the good money to be earned, the colourful characters that worked there, and the plentiful supply of girls of easy virtue. According to my informant, if you worked in Dreamland you didn't have to go chasing after girls – they came up and surrendered! I told Dennis all this over a cup of tea in Lyons Cafeteria, and by the time I'd finished we were discussing how we could get down to Margate and grab ourselves a piece of the action. The problem, as always, was funds. Dennis and I were both unemployed, woefully short of the wherewithal, and with no one to turn to for money. We were going to need enough for two single train fares, a week's rent in advance for our digs, and something to live on until we received our first pay-packet.

We reckoned that ten pounds would just about cover it, but where were we going to find that kind of money? *Any* kind of money, come to that?

The answer, or part of it, was on the third finger of my right hand. So desperate was I to get out of London that summer and work at the seaside, that I did a shameful thing. Heavy with guilt I entered the pledge department of W. Thompson's, the jewellers in Chalk Farm Road, took off the ring my mother had given me for my 21st, and asked the elderly pawnbroker how much he would advance me on it. After he'd examined it he offered me six pounds, after which I left, promising to return.

In order not to upset my mother the plan was that I would wear the ring right up to the day I left, stop off at the pawnshop on our way to Victoria Station, pawn the ring, and continue on our way to Margate. Then, on my return to London, I would redeem the pledge, and my mother would never know the ring had been off my finger. By the day of our departure we had managed to scrape together the extra four pounds we needed, and I was in high spirits as I re-entered the pledge department of W. Thompson's. They faded a little when I saw that I was being served by a different, younger man. I explained that I had been in a couple of weeks before and had been offered six pounds, and gave him the ring. He examined it for a moment, shook his head and grimaced. "Best I can do on this," he said, "is four pounds." My heart sank as I saw a large hole opening up in our carefully planned budget. After some desperate haggling he handed the ring back to me and said: "Four pounds ten shillings, top whack." I took the money and left. Out in the street Dennis and I took stock of the situation. The loss of thirty shillings was serious but not fatal. Anyway, we couldn't back out now, farewells had been taken, dies cast, bridges burnt. We decided the only way we could keep within our budget was to send our suitcases on ahead by rail, and hitch-hike down to Margate, which is what we did. After despatching our bags (to be collected at Margate Station) we took the underground to New Cross station, and set out to walk. It did occur to me that this wasn't really advisable just five months after leaving a TB Sanatorium, but I soon dismissed it from my mind. I was on my way to sun, sex and 'sovs' (money) and nothing was going to stop me now. The one thing we hadn't expected was not being able to get lifts easily. We should have realised, of course, that there are a lot of people – including lorry drivers – who are understandably reluctant to pick up *two* men, especially when it begins to get dark. As a result it was past midnight and we were just beyond Chatham. Knowing there wasn't much chance of progressing any further, we found a haystack in a field, covered ourselves with hay and went to sleep. I remember waking up at first light in a mist-shrouded landscape and seeing a large owl perched on a gatepost about ten feet away. The bird studied me for a moment, shook its head (in disbelief probably) and flew away.

In spite of our dishevelled appearance we quickly picked up a lift next day. Our luck was in. The driver was going all the way to Margate. Less than an hour later we were dropped off at the sea-front, on what turned out to be a sparkling sunny day. We found a cheap cafe, ate a large breakfast and, with spirits soaring, prepared to face the first day of our new venture. Things went well. By late afternoon we had found digs close to Dreamland Park (Bed, breakfast and evening meal, two pounds ten shillings a week each, sharing) retrieved our suitcases from Margate station, and set out to find the local billiard hall.

In those days almost all billiard halls were above a Burton's menswear shop, and Margate's was no exception. It was a 'find' in more ways than one, for it was there that most of the fairground workers, 'grafters' as they were called, would congregate. They gave us the names of several stall owners in Dreamland who were looking for staff. We played a couple of games of snooker, and decided on an early night.

The next day we were taken on by a man named Sid Leigh who had several joints (stalls) in the old arcade. We started off on a darts stall, then moved over to work on his Bingo. We worked six days a week, including every weekend, with one weekday off. We started at 10am, had an hour off for lunch and another hour off for tea, and worked until the Park closed at around 10pm. Then the Park Superintendant came on the public address system and announced: "Dreamland Park is now closing. Please make your way to the exits", followed by an ancient recording of 'When Day Is Done' played by Ambrose and his orchestra. There then followed a mad rush to get to the billiard hall or, more usually, to Dreamland Ballroom for the last hour and a half of the dance.

As the weeks went by it became increasingly clear that Dreamland was not quite the dream-world we had been led to believe. As we were working in a covered arcade the only sun we saw was on our day off, or at break times. Secondly, and much more importantly, the expected rush of girls throwing themselves at our feet begging for sex had not materialised.

It wasn't that the girls were not there. They were there alright, but most of them spent the day on the beach and then went dancing at night. What they *didn't* do was come into the arcade where we worked. On top of that the competition was petty fierce.

Apart from all the other grafters in the Park, there was also the American Air Force Base at Manston, three miles outside Margate, a situation that guaranteed demand would always outstrip supply.

The Yanks had plenty of money, wore the kind of civilian clothes we'd have given our eye teeth for, and talked like film stars. By the time we got to Dreamland Ballroom most of the girls had been chatted up and snapped up. The only part of the promise of sun, sex and sovs to come good so far had been the sovs.

However, all that was about to change the day Dennis and I met Pip and Tod. Almost everyone who worked in Dreamland at that time was a 'character', and Pip and Tod were two of them. Here are the names of some of others: Long Harry, Rainbow Jack, Trousers, Red-hand Sid, Fat Sid, One-ball Buster, Lino, Mad Percy, Fingers Phil, Derek the Cleric.

Some of the names are self-explanatory, but I think it's worth taking time to explain how the others came by their Runyonesque nicknames. Long Harry was six feet tall and weighed less than ten stone. He had been an army boxing champion, and had a steel plate in his head which was the result of a war wound. Because of this he had lost most of his hair, which he was very self-conscious about and always wore a trilby hat. He was a tough, uncompromising man with a hoarse cockney voice whose favourite word was 'diabolical'. Everything was diabolical for Harry, especially his luck when he was gambling. Rainbow Jack acquired his colourful name during the War. He was a fly-pitcher in the West End of London, selling all the things that were in short supply in wartime, such as nylon stockings, razor blades, number eight batteries etc, whilst always trying to keep one step ahead of the police. One day he was up at Marlborough Street Magistrate's Court for fly-pitching outside Rainbow Corner, a club for American servicemen in Piccadilly. During the proceedings Jack was intrigued to learn that the pavement outside the club was not a 'right of way' within the meaning of the act, apparently the pavement area belonged to the leaseholders, in this case the American government.

A few days later Jack pinned a borrowed row of medals on his coat, put a black glove on his left hand and held it stiffly to his side, put on a limp, went along to the American Embassy in Grosvenor

Square and asked to speak to the 'Guvnor'. After being shunted around for a while he was finally ushered into the office of someone in authority. Jack snapped him off a smart salute and went on to explain that he was an old soldier down on his luck, and that he would be very much obliged if they would give him permission to eke out his meagre army pension by selling a few bits and pieces outside their premises at Rainbow Corner. The official, totally taken in (and aback I shouldn't wonder) granted his request. Jack set up his stall on one of the best pitches in London, and the police couldn't touch him. That is the story of how Jack found his own personal rainbow.

'Trousers' was a tall, thin young man with a shambling gait and no discernable buttocks. As a consequence, his trousers were always slipping down, leaving the crotch between his knees and the bottoms of his trouser legs resembling two concertinas. Red-hand Sid had a 'strawberry' birthmark completely covering his left hand. 'Fingers' Phil had three fingers missing from his right hand. Conscious of the fact that when he shook hands with someone who didn't know him all they would be grasping were his forefinger and thumb, he would always say, 'Excuse the fingers' as he extended his hand. 'One-ball' Buster had one of his testicles bitten off by a dog when he was a toddler. He was playing naked in his back garden one summer day, went to stroke a stray dog, and ended up a semi-castrati. (I know you think I'm making this up, but it's all true, I promise) 'Lino' was so-called because when he tapped someone for money – which he did all the time – he would describe himself as being 'on the floor', his expression for being broke. As he *always* seemed to be on the floor, they called him Lino. Derek the Cleric had spent two years in a Catholic seminary studying to be a priest, before deciding that a celibate life was not for him. But to get back to Pip and Tod. Peter(Pip) Lee and Harry (Tod) Tondy were big men in every sense of the word, both standing over six feet tall and weighing in at around eighteen and sixteen stone respectively. They were two genial giants of great warmth and friendliness, with a huge appetite for food and gambling.

They worked on the 'smudge' (taking photographs) for the Carolan brothers on a pitch down by the coach park, next to the roller-skating rink.

On our way to lunch one day Dennis and I stopped to talk to them; a meeting that, for me, was the beginning of a life-long friendship, and for Dennis and myself a fortuitous and beneficial change of direction. The Carolans provided a while-u-wait service, delivering most photographs within the hour, and in the words of Pip they were 'having a burster'. In 1949 very few people had cameras, and if they did, film was in very short supply. Consequently the 'Get your souvenir of Dreamland' sales pitch worked very well, and earned them all good money.

Such was the volume of business, we were told, that the Carolans were thinking of taking on two more workers and opening another pitch up near the Hall of Mirrors, about thirty yards away. The upshot was that Pip introduced us to Trevor, his boss, who immediately offered us a job, which we both accepted with alacrity. The attractions of working on the 'smudge' were manifold: out in the sun all day, finishing work at around 6.30pm, and good basic pay and bonuses. The biggest plus for Dennis and I was that it gave us the opportunity to chat up girls, while talking them into having their photograph taken. Because it was a fast service we had to use old fashioned plate cameras mounted on tripods, which even in 1949 looked antiquated, but they were simple to operate and did the job.

Those were the boom years for seaside amusement parks. The cheap, foreign package holiday business was in its infancy, and after six years of War and austerity, people were out to enjoy themselves when they went on holiday. Back then Dreamland was an old fashioned, traditional fairground complete with: A Wall of Death, a Tunnel of Love, a Scenic Railway, a children's Zoo, fortune tellers, a Tattooed Man, a donkey ride, a roller-skating rink and a sideshow. The sideshow was directly opposite our photographic pitch, and each season featured a different attraction. One year it was a mind-reading act. The next, an exotic female dancer (with an *embonpoint* wondrous to behold) who finished her act with the Dance of the Seven Veils, to the strains of an ancient recording of Ravel's Bolero. Then, in 1952, we had an escapologist and fire-eater who claimed to be an American Indian. I have to say he *did* look the part, but I believe he actually came from Hoxton in London.

He had with him two assistants who were both dressed in buckskins, with painted faces and feathered head-dresses, whose job was to stand outside beating tom-toms whilst doing a clumsy imitation of an Indian war dance – all to attract the punters. One of them could just about pass muster as a Red Indian – but the other most definitely couldn't. He was very small of stature, with a gnome-like face dominated by huge thyroidal eyes. His name was Marty Feldman. I discovered this after chatting to him one day. I asked him, jokingly, which Red Indian tribe he was from. He said: "The Kishmeintuchas. I'm Little Big Horn; also known as Marty Feldman." During our chat he told me his aim was to break into show business. So I said: "Then what are you doing here?"

He shrugged, and said: "You've got to start *somewhere.*"

Many years later, in the late 1960's, I was in Ronnie Scott's Club in Soho, and Marty Feldman was there. He was now a very famous comedy writer and film actor. I introduced myself to him, and reminded him of his early days in 'show business' on a sideshow in Dreamland Amusement Park. He was delighted to see me, and we reminisced for a while as he remembered being the only Jewish Red Indian in the world.

> *"Bliss it was in that dawn to be alive,*
> *But to be young was very heaven"*

I was twenty one, good looking, with money to spend, and a lot of catching-up to do. I was out in the sunshine all day, and dancing to Joe Blake and his orchestra at night. Snogging on the beach or in nearby Dane Park (if wet, a seafront shelter). Winning some, losing some – it didn't matter. After almost two years of monastic self-denial *everything* was bright, fresh and exciting. Then, it happened. Out of a clear blue sky (literally) I fell in love for the first time. It was a quiet, hot afternoon in late August and Dreamland was deserted. I was sitting on a low wall in front of the roller-skating rink, reflecting sadly that the season was almost over, and the best three months of my life would soon be coming to an end. Then, out of the shimmering heat haze, I saw a young girl of transcendental beauty walking towards me.

She had short, dark hair, violet blue eyes, long, tanned legs, and was wearing a pair of shorts and a bathing suit top; revealing the kind of cleavage men used to fight duels over. Leaping to my feet I managed to stop her and take her photograph. During the chat-up afterwards I discovered that her name was Diane Boyce, she was 17 (and still at school) lived in Streatham in south west London, was staying in Broadstairs, and was going back to London on Saturday!! Throwing discretion to the wind I asked her if I could take her out that night. To my astonishment, she said yes. During those last few days of her holiday we spent every spare moment together, meeting in my lunch break and going out to eat every night, walking hand in hand along the seashore or up on the cliffs of Broadstairs.

By the time Diane was due to leave I was absolutely besotted, and had good reason to believe she felt the same way about me. Before she left she gave me her 'phone number, and I promised to ring her as soon as I returned to London. Dreamland Park closed down the second week in September. Pip and Tod were going up to Blackpool for the Illuminations and then on to Nottingham for the annual Goose Fair, and wanted Dennis and I to go with them. Dennis was keen, but so desperate was I to get back to see Diane again that I went straight back to London. I did see her of course, but nowhere near as much as I wanted, once or twice a week – if I was lucky. She was studying for exams, which meant devoting two or three evenings a week to revision. Also her parents socialised quite a bit and expected Diane to accompany them, usually making sure there was a presentable young man to escort her – or so it seemed. It wasn't that they disliked me, in fact I got on quite well with them.

It was simply that they probably considered a fairground worker, however nice, a not entirely suitable boy friend for their daughter, and the high expectations they had for her. There was also the marked difference in our backgrounds. Diane's father owned a car showroom in Croydon and drove a Rolls Royce. Diane attended a fee-paying college, and lived in a luxury apartment block. My dad was a painter and decorator and we lived on a Council estate.

On my return to London I had taken a job in an office. My high hopes of coming back with a stash of cash had not materialised. I had been far too intent on having a good time to save any money. I had just enough to get my ring out of hock, and that was it. The job was with a Mail-Order company in Kentish Town, where I was more or less the office boy on a wage of four pounds a week. Less than a third of the amount I had been earning in Dreamland, but I needed the money so I swallowed my pride and soldiered on.

As the weeks went by it became increasingly difficult for me to keep our romance alive. For one thing we didn't have a phone, so I had to go out to a call box to call Diane. Then I had to travel all the way over to Streatham on the number 68 bus, which took almost an hour each way. Then, when I got there, all I could afford was the cinema, and sometimes not even that.

As the festive season approached Diane was invited to dance, and asked me to accompany her. It was to be held at the Grosvenor House Hotel in Park Lane; and evening dress was 'optional'. Although I was eager to go it did present me with one big problem. What to wear? My one and only suit was almost four years old and had seen better days, I couldn't possibly wear that to such a 'posh do'. My first thought was to hire a dinner suit from Moss Brothers in Covent Garden, but that idea was dropped like a hot potato when I found it would cost me almost a week's wages - just for one night! There was only one thing for it, I would have to buy a new suit for the occasion, but where was the money to come from? The answer was - a Provident Cheque. 'Provident' cheques had been part of my life for almost as long as I could remember. When we were kids it was the only way my mother was able to buy us a new pair of boots or something to wear. You simply applied for a 'provvy', took it along to a participating store, and used it instead of cash.

The debt was cleared by weekly repayments, and interest was charged at 5% (a shilling in the pound). The provvy I took out was to the value of ten pounds, which I hoped would be enough to for a suit, and perhaps a new shirt and tie. For the past three or four weeks I had been going to a jeweller's shop in Camden Town paying weekly instalments on a powder compact I was buying for Diane as a Christmas present, and on the other side of the road there was a bespoke tailor, with a notice in the window indicating that they accepted Provident cheques.

So it was there, two weeks before the dance, that I went to be measured for a 'hand-made' suit. Having a limited choice of cloth in my price range I eventually settled for a brown, bird's-eye worsted, to be made up as a single breasted, two-piece suit. Big mistake! But that was just the beginning of the debacle. When I went to pick up the suit, the day before the dance, it didn't fit properly. The sleeves were a bit too long and it was too tight under the arms. But because there was now no time to do any alterations I was forced to take it – faults and all.

I can remember standing self-consciously in the foyer of the Grosvenor Hotel waiting for Diane to arrive, feeling (and no doubt looking) like a fish out of water. As far as I could see *all* the men were wearing dinner jackets. Mine was the only lounge suit – and an ill-fitting lounge suit at that. When Diane arrived, chauffeured by her father, she was wearing a white, low-cut, off the shoulder evening gown, and looked absolutely stunning, which only served to increase my extreme discomfort because of all the attention she was attracting.

I remember very little about that evening. I just wanted it to be over. When Diane's father arrived to pick her up it was past midnight and, because of the hour, he insisted on driving me home. As the Rolls pulled up outside Montague Tibbles House there were a group of drunks on the opposite corner, singing and swaying about. When I kissed Diane on the cheek before getting out of the car she gave me a wan, sad smile, and as the car drove off she was looking away.

I spoke to her on Christmas Day, but after that she always seemed to be out. I tried ringing her on New Year's Eve, but was told she had gone to a party.

1950 was only a few days old when I received a letter from her. In it she said she thought it best that we didn't see each other again, and that she would always remember me with affection...Like so many 'holiday romances' ours had failed to survive the journey back to reality.

The only consolation in losing someone you love when they are young is that their memory remains, like a photograph, fixed in time, unchanged and unchanging. In my mind's eye Diane is still 17, raven haired and breathtakingly beautiful. However time has passed and, if still with us, she will be now in her mid seventies, so I will close this chapter with Yeats' poem, When You Are Old...

"When you are old and grey and full of sleep,
And nodding by the fire, take down this book,
And slowly read, and dream of the soft look
Your eyes had once, and of their shadows deep.
How many loved your moments of glad grace,
And loved your beauty with love false or true,
But one man loved the pilgrim soul in you,
And loved the sorrows of your changing face,
And bending down beside the glowing bars,
Murmur, a little sadly, how Love fled
And paced upon the mountains overhead
And hid his face amid a crowd of stars."

The only glimmer of light in the gloom that followed our break-up was the prospect of going back to Margate again. So I stuck to my poorly paid, humdrum job, and counted the lingering days until Whitsun. It was in the Spring of 1950 that I saw my first stage play.

The Bedford theatre in Camden High Street had been a Variety theatre since the mid 1930's, but in 1949 Donald Wolfit, in what was perhaps an over-optimistic attempt to bring classical theatre to Camden Town, had taken over the theatre. One night, more out of curiosity than anything else, my cousin Jim and I paid one shilling and sixpence for a seat in the gods to see a play by George Du Maurier called Trilby, with Donald Wolfit playing Svengali.

It was a part 'tailor-made' for Wolfit; and he didn't disappoint. Incidentally, I have often heard it said that Donald Wolfit deliberately surrounded himself with inferior actors in order to enhance his own performance. I have always found that difficult to believe for the simple reason that he didn't need to. With that wonderful leonine head, his mellifluous voice and commanding stage presence you didn't look at anyone else when he was on stage anyway. What he *did* do though – and I have this on good authority – was to have the lighting kept on a slightly low-key until he made his first entrance; whereupon the lighting would gradually come up to full; giving the illusion that he 'lit up the stage' when he came on. Watching him on stage was a revelation to me, and a spur, because it was there, sitting in the gods of a dilapidated old theatre in Camden Town that I began to seriously consider the prospect of becoming an actor.

Some 15 years or so later I actually found myself working alongside Donald Wolfit, or *Sir* Donald as he was then. He was in his early sixties at that time and working in television, a medium he didn't much care for. It was a play with music entitled And Benbow Was His Name, with Sir Donald playing the eponymous eighteenth century Admiral, and directed by Ned Sherrin. I must say he cut a rather sad figure at that time. His suits (he always wore a suit) were old fashioned and rather frayed, and there was an air of faded grandeur about him. One day during a break in rehearsals I told him about the night in 1950 when I saw him play Svengali at the Bedford Theatre, and how it had spurred me on to become an actor. For some reason he seemed quite moved by my story and, to my embarrassment, went around telling the whole company about it. I say 'embarrassment' because the cast included John Wood and Paddy Newell, two actors who were both renowned for their wicked sense of humour. In no time at all they had put it about that I had made the whole thing up in order to curry favour with 'Sir'!

By Whitsun 1950, not having been as enamoured with fairground life as I, my cousin Dennis had decided against making the trip for the second time. So it was just Pip, Tod and I in the back of the Carolan's van, along with the cameras and darkroom equipment, as we headed across London towards Blackheath, and out onto the A2 to Margate. The summer of 1950 was virtually a re-run of the previous year, except that this time I palled-up with Jack Mitchell who had come to work with us. Although Pip and Tod were wonderful company they preferred the billiard hall to the ballroom, and the dog track to dancing. Jack was a kindred spirit, a snappy dresser with a Clark Gable moustache whose *raison d'etre* was to get his leg over as frequently as possible. We made a good double act.

And so another carefree season went by: sun, fun, dating and dancing. Sometimes it could get a bit hairy at weekends when coach-loads of drunken day - trippers descended on Dreamland, but apart from that the job was a doddle, and my winter of discontent soon turned glorious summer.

I decided that this was to be the pattern of my life for the foreseeable future. Take a job – any job – during the winter, then spend the summer in Margate. Not a very ambitious plan I suppose, but it would do until something better came along. For the 1951 season Pip and I had decided on a change, and had gone to work for a company called Sunbeam Photos. They were based in Cliftonville and had the photographic concessions for most of the piers, beaches and promenades on the Isle of Thanet. We worked as a team, Pip taking photos up on the pier with me down on the beach in a pair of shorts chatting up the girls. We earned more or less the same money as we would have in Dreamland, but it wasn't the same. We missed the characters and the camaraderie of the fairground, and after just one season away, went back to the Carolans.

CHAPTER 8

MONKEY BUSINESS

When I arrived in Margate for the summer season of 1952, change was in the air. Firstly, the Carolan brothers had decided that this was to be their last season in Dreamland. Secondly, I found to my dismay that my erstwhile pulling partner, Jack Mitchell, had got himself engaged in the interim, which meant his philandering days were over. And thirdly, I met the girl who was to become my first wife. Jack's fiancé lived in Ramsgate and had a girlfriend called Joan Long who, according to Jack, looked like Simone Signoret, was built like a brick oast-house, and was rather free with her favours. Being the pal that he was, he had shown her a photograph of me taken the year before, and waxed lyrical about what a splendid fellow I was, so much so that she had expressed a desire to meet me. Within a few days it was all set up. It was to be a blind date (well, not entirely blind, Joan having already seen a photo of me - a 'one-eyed' date perhaps) and we were to meet after I had finished work, at the East Kent Bus Stop at Ramsgate harbour. Not the most romantic of trysting places but a practical one, in that I had never been to Ramsgate before.

In her autobiography, Lady Don't Fall Backwards, Joan describes our meeting like this: "My date was standing on the platform as the bus pulled in, and as it slowed to a halt he leapt off. At my first sight of him, suspended as he seemed in mid-air, I knew why nobody else had won my heart. Fate had reserved it for him." For myself, I saw a beautiful face with a full, sensuous mouth, smiling brown eyes, and a figure of Junoesque voluptuousness. Over a cup of coffee in Pelosi's ice cream parlour in Queen Street I learned that she was 21 years old, worked as a dental nurse at a practice in Broadstairs, and that her father owned a fish shop in King Street. It didn't take me long to realise that Joan was markedly different to most other girls I had met. She had a quick wit, a razor-sharp sense of humour, and a throaty, infectious laugh. What is more, she was extremely well read and could quote from a wide range of poetry. This was all very interesting of course, but not what I had come over from Margate for. That journey had been made in the expectation of enjoying intercourse of the sexual variety, rather than the social kind. So, in pursuit of this ignoble end, I walked Joan up onto the west cliff, found a secluded spot, and settled down for some pre-coital wrestling. For the next hour we both fought valiantly for the same thing: her honour. But as time began to run out and the hoped-for submission had not materialised, I played one last trump card; Andrew Marvell's 'To his coy Mistress'. Laying particular emphasis on:

> *"Then worms shall try*
> *That long preserved virginity:*
> *And your quaint honour turn to dust;*
> *And into ashes all my lust."*

It didn't work, so I conceded defeat. When I eventually got to the bus stop, a quick glance at the timetable confirmed that I had missed the last bus. Determined not to add the cost of a taxi to what already been an unprofitable evening, I walked the three miles back to Margate. Before I left, Joan had given me her telephone number, but I didn't call, which will give you some indication of what a shallow, ungracious sort of fellow I was at that time.

One weekend, towards the end of the season, I became aware of a small, dark haired man watching me at work. After a while he came over and introduced himself. He told me his name was Eddie Mann, that he has acquired the photographic concession for the following year, and wanted to know if I would like to work for him? Offering me a couple of pounds more than I was getting with the Carolans, plus a generous weekly bonus. Without pausing to think it over, I accepted. "Oh, by the way," he said as we shook hands, "I hope you like animals, because you'll be working with monkeys."

Fast-forward to Whitsun, 1953. With the departure of the Carolans, Pip and Tod had decided on a change of direction, and had gone to run a Bingo in a small arcade in Cliftonville, so I arrived in Margate with my friend George Tinneny. George had been at a bit of a loose end since finishing his National Service and I had talked him into coming to work with me in Dreamland. We had gone down a week early to 'establish a rapport' with the monkeys!

From day one we both realised that a trying and troublesome time lay ahead. I was given a small, female monkey called Chrissie, who was fairly docile. George was given a much bigger male monkey named Jimmy, who was aggressive and difficult to handle. Monkeys are unpredictable creatures at the best of times, and amid the noise and confusion of a fairground they could easily become frightened and start biting people, especially Jimmy, who needed very little excuse to be a hooligan. It became especially nerve-racking if children were involved, as they often were, and we had to be constantly on our guard. It also raised the question of whether what we were doing actually amounted to cruelty to the animals. I rather think it did, but we were allowed to continue. There were, however, quite a few people who were bitten, shat upon, or peed over (sometimes all three) whilst having their photo taken with a monkey sitting on their shoulder, all of which created a great deal of stress for the punters - and for us. The compensation, as always, was money. That magic balm that soothes the troubled conscience, and stifles doubt.

One Saturday afternoon about halfway through the season, Joan came into Dreamland with a girlfriend. It was over a year since I had seen her, and she looked utterly delectable. I took her photograph and we talked. In no time at all my petulant behaviour of the previous summer had been forgotten, and we had made a date for that same evening. It was to be love at second sight. We spent the night together at Joan's flat in Ramsgate, and every other night from then on, leaving poor old George – whom I had dragged down to Margate in the first place – to his own devices.

By the end of that summer Joan and I had decided to get married and, in the first of many attempts to save money, I went up to London to buy a second-hand suit in which to get wed. There were two second-hand clothes shops in Camden Town at that time: a small one in Chalk Farm Road called Goode, Seck and Hand (honestly), and a much grander emporium in the High Street, a few doors up from the old Camden Hippodrome, called Alfred Kemp.

The big neon sign above the shop proclaimed 'Alfred Kemp Can Fit Anybody!', so I tried there first.

Twenty minutes later Alf's boast had been made good and I had been fitted out with a natty, blue pin-stripe, double breasted suit for the modest outlay of £3.10s (£3.50p) For reasons which, to this day I am unable to justify, I did not tell my mum and dad I was getting married. I had some foolish idea that because it was to be a civil marriage my parents, being devout Catholics, would refuse to attend or try to talk me out of it. As it happened I was wrong on both counts, which only goes to show how little I knew about my parents.

On Saturday 23rd of October 1953 Joan and I were married at Ramsgate Registry Office, with George as my best man. My bride wore a green, tweed suit with a black feathered hat, and I wore my recent acquisition from the Alfred Kemp Collection. Apart from George, Jack Mitchell and his (now) wife, all the other guests were from Joan's family. The reception was held at 119 King Street, Joan's parent's house. My new in-laws put on a grand spread, and a good time was had by all.

However, not everyone was delighted at our union. Joan's employer, a snobbish little Broadstairs dentist, had been horrified when he learned that his nurse was to marry a fairground worker, had forbidden her to mention it to any of his patients and continued to address her as 'Miss Long' until the day she left. Also, one of Joan's friends wrote to someone that Joan had 'married an out-of-town spiv'.

However, Joan's family liked me, so that was a good start.

> *"Need we expose to vulgar sight,*
> *The raptures of the bridal night?*
> *Need we intrude 'pon hallowed ground,*
> *or pull the curtains closed around?"*
> *Suffice to say that each had charms,*
> *He held a goddess in his arms;*
> *And tho' she felt his usage rough,*
> *In a man 'twas well enough."*

Actually it wasn't like that at all on our wedding night. We had rented two furnished rooms in a house on the east cliff, sharing a bathroom and loo with the flat below. When we got back there on our wedding night Joan, who was feeling a bit squiffy, took herself off to bed, so I sat down and wrote a long letter to my parents explaining, as best I could, what I had done and why, and asking their forgiveness.

As the weeks passed and there was no reply I realised how deeply hurt they must have been at my stupidity, and that there was going to be a lot of bridge-building to do. I also realised that there would have to be a lot of readjustment on my part as well. I had to live by different rules now and had new responsibilities. Was I going to be up to it, I asked myself? Alas, the answer was to be – no. All too soon I would begin to feel trapped, stifled and tied down.

But that was all in the future. At the moment we were young and in love, and planning our future together. Eager eyes forever scanning the far horizon for the ship that might, one day, come in for us. One of my first steps was to get a job. Ramsgate was a ghost town during the winter months and there was very little work available, but Joan's uncle Harry, bless his heart, 'put in a good word' for me at the small plastics factory where he worked, and got me a job in the despatch department.

It was tedious, repetitive work, but that didn't bother me. What I did find hard to accept though was the dictatorial attitude of the management and the subservience of the workforce. But the pay was £6 a week and we desperately needed the money, so I swallowed my pride and kept my lip buttoned...until the day before Christmas. Before we left for the Christmas break we were summoned to a pep-talk from the managing director, a Mr Cole. He began by reminding us how lucky we were to have a job in what was a depressed area, and went on to imply that unless we all put our noses to the collective grindstone and improved productivity, some of us might well be out of a job in the new year.

To my astonishment, when he had finished speaking the assembled workforce gave him a round of sycophantic applause. Unable to control my anger I said loudly: "Thank you, Mr Cole. When you call round again we'll be glad to throw you on the fire." In the deathly hush that followed my outburst I caught a glimpse of Uncle Harry. He looked like a man about to face a firing squad. Mr Cole spoke briefly to the factory manager, then turned and left.

I had been sacked on the spot. Joan was understanding and supportive, but we both knew that because of my irresponsibility, hard times were on their way. There were almost six months to go before the start of the summer season, and no other work was available. Joan's wage was £4 a week and my dole money was £2.15s (£2.55p) so making ends meet was going to be an uphill struggle. Fred and Nellie, my in-laws, helped us out whenever they could with a piece of fish or some vegetables from Fred's allotment, but they were almost as strapped as we were, only opening the fish shop on Fridays and Saturdays. We survived because our needs were, perforce, simple. We seldom drank, rationed ourselves to five cigarettes a day, and went to the cinema once a week - in the cheapest seats.

CHAPTER 9

THE SEED IS SOWN

At long last, away in the distance, a small cloud of dust appeared. It was the Seventh Cavalry, flags flying and bugles blowing, riding to the rescue... the summer season had arrived. Because of the barrage of complaints from the previous year, Eddie Mann was not offered the photographic concession for 1954, and Sunbeam had taken over. Having already worked for them in 1952 I was taken on again, this time working the pitch single-handed. It was hard but rewarding and for the first time in my life I was putting money away. By the time the season came to an end Joan and I had managed to save just over £100 pounds, a substantial sum at that time.

By early 1955 Fred and Nellie had decided to move away from Ramsgate. It was a heart-wrenching decision for them both. Fred had been born and bred in Ramsgate, and he and Nellie had spent almost their entire married life there, but they had had enough of working for just three months of the year then struggling to get by for the remaining nine. They put down a deposit on a house in a newly-built estate near Dunstable, packed all their furniture and belongings into a hired van, and accompanied by Joan's two brothers David and Terry, drove up to Luton. Not the most salubrious or picturesque of towns perhaps, but at that time the hub of the British car industry with plenty of jobs on offer.

Joan and I took over their house at 119 King Street, paying them thirty shillings (£1.50p) a week rent. We used part of our savings to furnish it, and for the first time had a home of our own. I bought a piano at the local auction rooms for twenty five shillings (£1.25p) and began to practice again. Within a few months I was good enough to get a weekend job playing in a pub.

Sadly, by 1956 the strands of our marriage had begun to unravel. Our lovemaking, which had once been so joyful and fulfilling, had slowly faded away and we were living more like brother and sister than man and wife. I don't think there was any one reason, or anyone's fault; it just happened. Although in her autobiography Joan blamed herself; this is what she wrote: "There was still an enormous affection between us, lots of hugging and kissing, until it began to get serious, then I would cry off. Gradually, making love became one of my nightly chores, like bathing or brushing my teeth, and there was always the same feeling of sadness when it was over. I don't know why, but with marriage somehow the glamour had gone...Mercifully it didn't diminish our love and friendship for each other. It was, however, the cause of many arguments, and created a gulf between us that eventually led to our parting."

In the latter part of that year, after another summer working as a photographer in Dreamland, two landmark events occurred. In September Joan discovered she was pregnant, and in November the Everyman Amateur Drama Group offered me the role of Thomas Mendip in Christopher Fry's, The Lady's Not for Burning. Both of which left me stunned with amazement – and incredulity. Joan and I had made love for the first time in six months and she had conceived! I had joined the drama group only a few weeks previously, mainly for something to occupy me during the long winter months, and now they were offering me the leading role in their next production! Although I was extremely flattered to be asked, upon reading the play my first reaction was to say no. It was a very long part, and written in blank verse. A daunting prospect for a seasoned actor, let alone someone who had last set foot on a stage fifteen years earlier playing Fourth Townsperson in a school production of The Pied Piper of Hamelin, with just one line to say!

It was Joan who talked me into doing it, an act of faith on her part for which I will be forever grateful. She had the confidence in my ability that I lacked, and it was at her insistence that I accepted.

Throughout the long rehearsal period she was a tower of strength. Night after night she would take me through my lines, correcting, suggesting and encouraging. She willed me to succeed – and I did. The opening night in mid January 1957 was a small triumph. The next day The East Kent Times gave us a rather good notice, and the five-night run was a sellout. As we took our bows at the end of the last performance I knew without any doubt where my future lay. I was going to be an actor.

That summer I took a job as a Bingo caller in Merrie England, a small fairground on the seafront in Ramsgate, to be close at hand for the arrival of our first-born. On the morning of the 9th of June Joan started to have contractions and I took her to Ramsgate General Hospital in a taxi. On the following day at around 8.30pm, after a protracted and painful labour, our son David was born. When the telephone call came through, I ran all the way to the hospital up on the west cliff and held him in my arms until it was time to leave.

The following September I left for London on the first step of my journey towards becoming an actor. I went with Joan's blessing, even though she must have known in her heart, as I did, that in spite of now having a son, the bonds of our marriage had begun to loosen and that we would eventually drift apart. She also knew that I would always bitterly regret never having tried to realise my ambition, so she let me go, putting my interests before her own. I loved and admired her for that, and after all these years I still do. She is a truly remarkable woman: generous, passionate, compassionate, funny and outrageous. Not the best judge of character perhaps, but a big-hearted life-enhancer, whose bonnet has sailed over more windmills than you've had hot dinners!

I arrived in London with absolutely no idea how to go about becoming an actor. I had long since made it up with my parents who, as always, were putting me up rent free until something came along, and my sister Kathleen was now a student at The Rose Bruford College of Speech and Drama in Kent, which was a help – but not much. It was she who advised that the only way for me to gain a foothold in the acting profession was to start at the bottom - as an assistant stage manager in one of the many repertory companies, adding that it was hard, and at times, thankless work. But as I was working temporarily as a builder's labourer at the time that didn't really bother me. Every week I bought 'The Stage' and scanned the Situations Vacant columns for something that might be suitable but to no avail... until, just before Christmas an advertisement appeared that ignited a small flame of hope. John Chilvers announced that he would be coming to London early in the New Year to audition actors for the upcoming season at the Grand Theatre, Swansea. Also he would be auditioning for one ASM (female) *and one ASM (male)*! Please apply enclosing photograph etc.

Fortunately we knew a chap who was a keen amateur photographer and lived just across the road from us. That evening I paid him a visit. After explaining the situation to him he very kindly offered to do me some 'stills' for a nominal fee, and because he did his own developing and printing they were ready by the next day.

When I sat down to write to John Chilvers I had already decided to change my name; the main reason being superstition. Firstly, no one in our family had *ever* had one single stroke of good fortune in their entire lives, so I thought a change of name might bring a change of luck. Secondly, in French the un-capitalized word malin means malignant. Irrational I know, but I was entering a profession in which superstition is deep-rooted. I had always liked the name Mark, and there had been a lot in the papers recently about Anthony Eden the ex Prime Minister, so I chose that as my surname. It was quite by chance that my initials now spelt ME.

About a week later, to my surprise, I received a reply from John Chilvers asking me to come to The Spotlight offices in Leicester Square early in the New Year for an interview, with a prepared audition piece. I had cleared the first hurdle. For my audition piece I had chosen a short speech from The Lady's not for Burning. It was this one:

*"Just see me as I am. A perambulating vegetable, looking out of two small
jellies for the means of life. Balanced on folding bones, my sex no beauty
but a blemish, to be hidden behind judicious rags. I defend myself against
pain and death, by pain and death. And make the world go round, they tell
me, by one of my less lethal appetites. Half this grotesque life I spend in a
state of slow decomposition, using the name of unconsidered God as a
pedestal, on which I stand and bray that I am the best of beasts. Until,
under some patient moon or other, I fall to pieces like a cake of dung."*

Considering how nervous I was, I did it quite well. John Chilvers
must have thought so too because he offered me the job there and
then: ASM playing small parts on a salary of £7 a week. I was on my
way!

CHAPTER 10

HI-DIDDLE-DE-DEE,
AN ACTOR'S LIFE FOR ME

When I arrived in Swansea on the 8th of February 1958 it was snowing, so I took a taxi to the theatre. My intention was to study the digs list which I was told I would find in the Green Room, and find myself somewhere to stay. As I was finding my way around backstage I bumped into John Chilvers. "Why don't you try Mrs Thomas in Argyle Street?" he said. "I believe she's very good."

She was more than very good, she was a gem of purest ray serene, a sweet, motherly woman with two grown-up daughters, who treated me like a son, cooking me wonderful meals, leaving cold collations in my room when I was working late, and doing my washing and ironing. And all for £3.10shillings (£3.50p) a week.

Dear Mrs Thomas, I bless your memory still. On the first Monday morning we all gathered on stage to meet each other and to read through the first play; and from the moment I was introduced to Tom Bell I knew we would be friends, which we were and remained so until his death in 2006.

As soon as I started work any illusions I had about the 'glamour' of working in the theatre were quickly dispelled. I had been forewarned that weekly rep would be hard going, but what I hadn't bargained for was the long hours I was expected to put in. I found myself arriving at the theatre in the morning long before anyone else, and invariably I was the last one to leave at night. Performing one play at night and rehearsing another during the day was difficult enough for the actors. For the stage management it was gruelling, especially for me. I had had no experience of backstage work whatsoever and had to learn the hard way – by trial and error as I went along. What I found particularly difficult was when I had a part to play, which was almost every week! Making a dignified exit on one side of the stage, then haring round to the prompt corner to activate a sound effect or give a lighting cue. Consequently, for the first couple of weeks I was in a state of nervous and physical exhaustion.

But it was weekends that were the most hectic. When the curtain came down on Saturday night, after two performances, stage management would begin to strike the old set (dismantle the scenery) and start to put up the new one. We would usually work until midnight, then come back at midday on Sunday and work through until the new set was up. Monday morning was spent returning hired furniture and props, picking up new ones, and then 'dressing' the set (putting up pictures, curtains etc, and laying the carpets). Monday afternoon was taken up with the technical and dress rehearsals, which sometimes went on so long that there was no opportunity to get a bite to eat or even a cup of tea before the opening evening performance.

To be honest, I am making it sound much worse than it was. Once I had got into the swing of things I did manage to get some time of and relax. And with the kindness of Mrs Thomas, the generosity of Tom (and by pinching a handful of prop cigarettes now and again) I managed to get by financially, sometimes even managing to send some money to Joan. Before I leave Swansea – as I was to do after just three months – I must tell you about a stunt Tom and I pulled one night which, now I think about it, perhaps went beyond the boundaries of good taste and acceptability. In the cast there was a charming character actress whose name I have forgotten, who I shall call 'Margaret'. She had been in the business for some time and always boasted that nobody had ever, *would* ever, make her 'corpse' (laugh involuntarily, or break up on stage) So Tom and I decided to put her to the test.

One week we were doing a play called The Rainmaker which was set in the American west in an area suffering from a prolonged drought. Margaret was playing the unmarried, middle-aged daughter of a rancher, who at one point in the play had to throw open the back door and cry out to the heavens: "Oh Lord, when will we have some rain?" One night Tom and I, both dressed as cowboys, positioned ourselves directly in her eye-line, but out of sight of the audience. As she flung open the door and wailed: "Oh Lord, when will we have some rain?" we were standing there, with our dicks out, pretending to pee into our Stetsons. Collapse of the un-corpsable Margaret!

Incidentally, Tom and I are among the small group of actors who can say they have played The Empire, Tonypandy. An amateur company had booked the Grand for a week and John Chilvers had, heaven knows why, fixed us a week in Tonypandy with a play called Cosh Boy. It was a charming place though. Sheep roamed the streets and gardens unmolested, and the inhabitants still spoke wistfully of Tommy Farr (British heavyweight boxing champion, 1935/1938) Tonypandy's most famous son. When we got to the theatre we found that it had been a cinema for the past 30 years, so you can imagine what it was like backstage. But it was early spring, the Rhondda was looking exceptionally beautiful, the people were welcoming and the weather was fine. What more could one ask?

Well, audiences for one thing, one night we played to just six people!

Towards the end of April I went to see John Chilvers and asked to be taken off stage management and re-engaged as an actor. How I had the temerity to make such a suggestion after just three months in the theatre never ceases to amaze me. My excuse is that I was a (not so) young man in a hurry, very eager to gain more experience *as an actor*. When John Chilvers politely declined my request, pointing out that he already had a full compliment of actors, I handed in my obligatory four weeks notice. Afterwards, as I made my way to a nearby cafe for a nerve-calming cup of tea I was thinking: what now?

Once again, fate took a hand. In The Stage that very week was an advertisement announcing that Jonathan Goodman would soon be auditioning for a full company to play the forthcoming summer

113

season at the Grand theatre, Llandudno. Please apply in writing enclosing recent photograph...etc, etc. I immediately sent off a letter applying for the position of juvenile lead; giving the Grand as my return address. Within a few days I received a reply asking me to meet Jonathan Goodman at the same Spotlight interview room I had met John Chilvers four months previously. I left Swansea towards the end of May, quite pleased with what I had achieved. I was now a 'provisional' member of Equity (the actors union) and had gained valuable practical experience working backstage.

When I met Jonathan Goodman I omitted to mention that I had been an ASM in my previous job, and when he asked what parts I had been playing I reeled off some of the roles Tom Bell had been given, which I think must have impressed him because he offered me the job of juvenile lead at a salary of £10 pounds a week.

Before going to Llandudno I managed to get down to Ramsgate to see Joan and David, who was now 11 months old. Joan had been thinking of taking in two lodgers during the summer months to help pay the bills when, by one of those happy coincidences, she had met Pip and Tod who were coming to Ramsgate to work in Merrie England and were looking for somewhere to stay. The upshot being that they both stayed with Joan, bringing in some much-needed extra cash, at least for a few months.

When I arrived in Llandudno the good fortune that had attended me thus far was to continue. I had picked Mrs Roberts name from the digs list because her house was only five minutes walk from the theatre, and her terms were £4 a week, full board. As it turned out, Mrs Roberts was another gem, cooking wonderful meals and making sure I had a freshly laundered shirt every day. The Grand Theatre Llandudno had opened in the mid 1890's had been saved from the ignominy of becoming a Bingo Hall by a wonderfully eccentric gentleman-farmer named John Creese-Parsons, who bred prize-winning bulls, had an abiding love of the theatre, and who was there at the Stage Door on the first morning of rehearsals to greet us.

On my arrival I noticed two theatrical skips at the side of the stage labelled 'Ian Shand. Grand Theatre. Llandudno'. Ian was to be our leading man and I must say I was really impressed. *Two skips* of clothes!

I looked at my one battered old suitcase and realised I had a bit of catching up to do in the wardrobe department. Apart from that I was pleased with what I had achieved. In little more than four months in the profession, with no formal training and little acting experience, I was a leading actor in a repertory company, with two of my photographs in the foyer, and installed in the No.1 dressing room! I have to come clean. The only reason I was in the No.1 dressing room was that it was rather small, and the leading man and leading lady had vast amounts of clothes to accommodate.

Also I was obliged to share it with another actor, an elderly thespian named Keith Shepherd. He was 82 years old and, as a child, had been taken to see Sir Henry Irving on stage. He also remembered gas footlights, and knew the history and origins of most theatre lore and superstitions. He was a fascinating man with a wry sense of humour and a fund of wonderful theatrical stories. He was also rather deaf, which presented a problem when he was on stage and 'dried' (forgot his lines) because he couldn't hear the prompt. If he 'dried' irretrievably he would suddenly say – apropos of nothing – 'I'll just go and get the nutcrackers' and walk off stage, leaving his fellow actors standing around in jaw-clenching, anus-contracting panic until he had elicited his next line from the prompter and come back on stage again, needless to say *without* any nutcrackers.

That summer of 1958 was a happy one for me. Llandudno is a pleasant seaside town surrounded by majestic mountain scenery. The choice of plays was varied and imaginative. We played to full, appreciative audiences most nights and I had an affair with one of the actresses in the cast. Unfortunately, romances that blossom in rep companies or in touring productions are rather like holiday romances, in that they seldom survive the return to reality. Sadly, ours was to prove no exception. The passion that had burned so brightly in Llandudno dwindled and finally died in London. The season ended at the end of September, after four months and sixteen different plays. And although, once again, the experience had been invaluable I had come to a decision. I would do no more weekly rep. Three weekly, or even two weekly at a pinch, but my weekly rep days were over. It was time to move on.

My first priority upon returning to London was to get an agent. If you wanted to do television work, which I did, a good agent was essential; so I aimed high. I sent a letter and photograph to Derek Marr, an up-market agent with offices in Baker Street, asking if he would care to represent me. He wrote back asking me to come and see him, which I did and was taken on. Within weeks I had my first television part. It was for the BBC in a serial called Quatermass and the Pit. I played Second Reporter with only three lines to say, for a fee of ten guineas, but it was a start.

Several other TV parts followed in quick succession, none of them amounting to more than 'a cough and a spit', but I was earning money.

Unable as yet to afford a place of my own I was, once again, living at home with my parents. It was a great help financially but it lacked that most essential of lifelines for an actor, a telephone. Through the actor's grapevine I heard about a theatrical club in Soho that would take, and pass on, telephone messages. It was called The Interval Club and was situated at 22/23 Dean Street. It was mainly, though not exclusively, for Catholic actors and actresses, and was run by a remarkable woman called Molly Belvoir-Hewitt. Molly was a lady of advancing years and failing eyesight, but possessed of great energy and doughty determination. It was a residential club as well. The terms were 3 pounds 10 shillings a week, full board, right in the centre of London!

Needless to say the waiting list for accommodation was as long as your arm. The membership fee was £5 a year, which you could pay in instalments if you wished. The restaurant was cheap and very good, and they were meticulous about passing on phone messages. So I joined. On my first day I was introduced to the inimitable, irreplaceable, unsinkable Ken Parry, lady of quality, clairvoyant, and 'mother' to a whole generation of actors, many of whom have good reason to remember his kindness and generosity. It was a friendship that was to last for almost 50 years until his sudden death in December 2007.

Among the acting profession stories about Ken Parry are legion, and we all have our favourites. This is mine. Kenny was up in Manchester doing a programme called Nearest and Dearest, a North Country sit-com starring a 4ft 10 inch virago named Hilda Baker. Miss Baker, as she insisted on being called, was difficult – one might almost say *impossible* - to work with. She invariably arrived late, threw tantrums, and ranted and raved, causing all sorts of headaches for her fellow actors, and long hold-ups for the production team. One morning however, to everyone's astonishment, Hilda came into rehearsal early, smiled at everybody, spoke softly, enquired after everyone's wellbeing, and was sweetness personified. During the lunch break the producer, Bill Podmore, and some of the cast were sitting together in the canteen, where the main topic of conversation was what could possibly have happened to have wrought this near miraculous transformation on Miss Baker.

"It's because," said Bill jokingly, "I went round to her hotel room last night and gave her a good 'seeing-to'." When the laughter had subsided Ken, with exquisite timing, said archly: "*I* can be difficult too, you know?" And set the table at a roar.

Just before Christmas 1958 I went down to Ramsgate to see Joan and David. I was anxious to see my son again, now an 18 month old delightful little lad, but there was another, more serious reason for my visit. I had come to tell Joan that our marriage was over. The fact that Joan had been half expecting it did nothing to soften the blow, but the tears when they came, sprang not from anger or a sense of betrayal, but from sadness and a sense of loss. There were no recriminations, only regret. The fact that our friendship and affection for each other has survived the break up is due entirely to Joan, and the understanding and forbearance she has always shown.

At the beginning of March 1959 I went along to see Dennis 'Slim'

Ramsden about a part in a play he was to direct. It was Arthur Miller's A View from the Bridge, which had just been granted a licence after being banned for over a year by the Lord Chamberlain on the grounds that the so-called 'kiss' in Act Two between two men might 'tend to deprave and corrupt'. It sounds laughable now of course, but it was not the least bit funny at the time. It was to be a prestigious 'Number One' tour under the auspices of Howard and Wyndham, a big West End management. Archie Duncan and Joan Rice were the two leads, and I was being considered for the part of Marco, a strong supporting role.

After doing a good reading, and waiting on tenterhooks for a couple of days, I learned that I had got the part! I was get third billing, and a salary of £20 pounds a week. After a three week rehearsal, we set off on a ten week tour. As soon as the train had pulled out of Euston station on the first leg of our journey, Joan Rice dropped me a hint that I had found favour with her. We were sitting in a four-seater with Slim Ramsden and Archie Duncan, playing cards, when she slipped her stockinged foot into my crotch, under the table, and wiggled her toes! Well I can take a hint – no matter how subtle; and so began a joyous, exhilarating tour in a brilliant play the whole country had been waiting to see. We packed them in, winning excellent reviews everywhere we went. Some nights we were even awarded a standing ovation! When the tour finally came to an end Joan and I made our farewells the night before and, by agreement, returned to London by different trains the next day. Sadly, our paths never crossed again. Joan Rice died on January 1st 1997, aged 66.

There is a story about 'tour' romances which is probably apocryphal – possibly not, but worth re-telling. It concerns a famous old Shakespearean actor named Godfrey Tearle who, in his time, had been a critically acclaimed Hamlet, and who also had the reputation of being a 'Ladies man'. In his latter years he was approached by a young actor who was about to play the doomed Dane, for some advice and guidance. After chatting for a while the young man asked Godfrey Tearle one last question: "Do you think Hamlet slept with

Ophelia?" His reply was: "Well I always did. (Slight pause) Only while we were on tour, of course."

I was not out of work for very long. Almost immediately I was offered a part in a new Agatha Christie play called Go Back for Murder, to be directed by Hubert Gregg, and destined for the West End. The drawback was, it was a small part in a not very good play and involved understudying the lead, but I took it because it would be my first West End appearance and, if it ran, would provide me with a regular wage for a while. It was not to be. After a brief pre-London tour we opened at the Duchess Theatre in mid July – and closed three weeks later after a panning from the critics. Within a month my agent had put me up for a part in another play bound for the West End. It was a comedy based on an award-winning TV series called You Prove It. The stars were to be Ronald Shiner and Thora Hird and it was to be directed by Gilchrist Caulder.

Ronald Shiner was a big 'name' at that time. He had appeared in virtually all the famous, long-running Whitehall farces of the forties and fifties, and had been a permanent fixture in British comedy films for years. Thora Hird was, well, Thora Hird, the wonderful character actress we all knew and loved, and although the script didn't exactly sparkle, I thought we could survive on star-power alone. I was wrong. Ronnie Shiner was then in his mid sixties and suffering from a chronic bronchial problem that would sometimes leave him fighting for breath on stage, while we stood agonisingly by willing him to recover.

Hold ups like that, in what was a fast-moving comedy were fatal, and the pre-London tour was not a happy one.

It was during that pre-London tour (and rapidly gaining in self-confidence) that I found myself in disagreement with the star of our show. I was playing Thora Hird's Teddy-boy son, and I had one scene with Neil McCarthy which was, arguably, one of the funniest in the play. Unfortunately, it took place just before Ronnie's first entrance; which rather tended to overshadow *his* first scene. We were playing the Hippodrome in Coventry, and just before the show on the second night Gilchrist Caulder came into my dressing room to tell me the scene between Neil and myself had been cut. He made some excuse about tightening up the show, but I knew the real reason, and I was furious. Not only because it was my best scene, but because it was a *funny* scene; and we needed all the laughs we could get.

After the show I knocked on Ronnie Shiner's dressing room door intending to make my feelings known. When I entered he was sitting at his dressing table, still in his stage make up, with a large glass of whiskey in his hand. Before I could say anything he said to me: "I know why you're here." When I asked him why he had cut my scene he looked at me sadly for a moment, then said: "Mark, let me explain something to you.

If this play flops in London it won't make a scrap of difference to you. You are a talented young actor, you'll walk away from it and go on to better things; but for me it will be the end. It's *my* name up there above the title and if this play fails, I fail. At my age I would probably never work in the West End again. It would be curtains for Ronnie Shiner."

Suitably chastened, I just said: "Fair enough." As I turned to go Ronnie said: "Don't go. Stay and have a drink with me."

He then opened what appeared to be a medium-sized leather suitcase, but in fact was a well stocked, miniature bar. I declined the drink and started to leave. As I turned to close the door behind me Ronnie was sitting staring at his reflection in the mirror, a look of bemused melancholy on that famous old face of his. Three weeks later we opened at the St. Martin's Theatre, got lambasted by the critics, and closed six weeks later. As far as I know, Ronnie Shiner never worked again after that.

CHAPTER 11

THE ROYAL COURT THEATRE

As 1959 came to an end I was still looking for that elusive 'big break' that every actor fondly imagines is waiting just around the corner. When it came, it happened, as important events sometimes do, by accident. It was simply a case of being in the right place at the right time. By 1960 the most exciting place to be for most young actors (and the not so young) was the Royal Court Theatre in Sloane Square. The Fringe as we know it today was in its infancy, and the National Theatre was still a strike-bound, half-finished building on the left bank.

It was the 'Court' that was the epicentre of all that was experimental, controversial, and innovative in the theatre of that period, and bristling with exciting, radical directors such as George Devine, Lindsey Anderson, John Dexter, Bill Gaskill, Peter Gill and Anthony Page among others. It was also the place where new and untried writers could get their plays put on.

One of the big successes of 1959 had been Willis Hall's play The Long and the Short and the Tall. It had started out at the Royal Court, directed by Lindsey Anderson, with a stellar cast of young actors including Peter O'Toole, Robert Shaw and Edward Judd.

After its initial run at the Court it had transferred to the New Theatre (now the Noel Coward) where it played to full houses for nine months to great acclaim, bringing stardom to all in the cast.

When the West End run came to an end there was a scramble among rep companies to put it on. One of the first was the Richmond Theatre. It was to be directed by Anthony Page, assistant to Lindsey Anderson on the original production, and every young actor in

London wanted to be in it. There were several reasons for this. The Richmond Theatre is only a short distance from central London, making it easily accessible to casting directors, agents, producers etc. All the parts are so well written that you couldn't really fail in any of them, but more importantly, it was being directed by one of the Royal Court's brightest stars, of whom great things were predicted.

I had originally gone up for the part of Private Bamforth, but when I was offered the role of Sergeant Mitchum, I jumped at it.

The cast Anthony Page put together way back then was one which, if it were possible to re-assemble today, would cost slightly more than the fifteen pounds a week we all received at the time. Terence Stamp, fresh from drama school in his first stage part, Harold Pinter, on the verge of international acclaim as a playwright, then an actor working under the name of David Baron. Also in the line up were Jack Smethurst, who was to find fame in television comedy, and Ian McNaughton who went on to become a prominent TV director.

A week before we opened I wrote to six or seven casting directors asking them to come and see me in the play. In the event only one came; Miriam Brickman. Miriam was the casting director for the Royal Court, a kind, shrewd, supportive woman who was brilliant at her job. Nowadays almost all casting directors are women, but Miriam was one of the first and one of the best. A great many actors owe their career breaks to Miriam – and I am me one of them.

The combination of a powerful play, a strong cast and brilliant direction ensured that The Long and the Short and the Tall would be a success, which it was. During the run my family came to see the play. It was the first time any of them had seen me on stage, and they were all very proud of me, especially my dad.

When the run of the play came to an end I dropped in to see Miriam one morning at her little prefab office round the back of the Royal Court. Miriam had made us a cup of tea and we were sitting chatting when the phone rang. From the conversation that ensued, I gathered that there was a crisis of some kind concerning The Wesker Trilogy, the first play of which was scheduled to open in six weeks time. When Miriam came off the phone she told me the full story. The actor Harry Landis, who had been cast as Dave Simmonds in the Trilogy, had been refused his (expected) release from the West End play he was appearing in at the time. That meant that, with rehearsals starting in a week's time, the part would have to be re-cast – and quickly. After that, the dialogue between us went something like this:

ME: Am *I* right for the part?
MIRIAM: Yes.
ME: Will you put me up for it?
MIRIAM: I can't. Arnold Wesker has insisted that the part has to be played by a Jewish actor.
ME: Well, tell them I told you I was Jewish.
PAUSE.
MIRIAM: Come back at two o'clock. I'll see what I can do. Now get out of here; I've got work to do.

When I returned at the appointed hour, Miriam thrust two sheets of paper into my hand. It was part of a scene from I'm Talking about Jerusalem, the third play in the trilogy. "Go away and have a look at it," she said, "then come back at three o'clock to read for John Dexter and Arnold Wesker." Bless her heart, she had got me the audition!

Dave Simmonds was a character based on Arnold Wesker's brother-in-law, who made a brief appearance in the first play, Chicken Soup with Barley, didn't appear in Roots, but was the leading role in I'm Talking about Jerusalem. For the next hour I sat on a bench in Sloane Square poring over the text.
Having worked in Dreamland with Pip and Tod, both East End Jewish boys, I tried to remember their speech patterns and cadences to use in my audition.

I went back at three o'clock, heart thumping. I was introduced to John Dexter and Arnold Wesker by Miriam, went up onto the stage and read the scene. I was then asked to read another scene, sight unseen, with Arnold Wesker himself, which I did.

After a brief, sotto voce conversation between John Dexter and Arnold Wesker, they thanked me for coming and said they would let me know, one way or the other, before seven pm that same day. When I looked down at Miriam who was sitting in the front row of the stalls, she gave me a conspiratorial wink.

I was still using the Interval Club as my telephone number, so I went back there and waited for the call that could, quite literally, change my life. That call came through at around 6.30pm. Miriam was delighted to tell me I had got the part, and to call in tomorrow morning and pick up the scripts. That was how, by a combination of incredible good fortune and my own ability, I came to be part of one of the most eagerly anticipated theatrical events of 1960, working in a company that included Joan Plowright, Frank Finlay, Alan Howard, Charles Kaye, Patsy Byrne, Kathleen Michael and David Saire.

Chicken Soup with Barley opened on 7th of June, and Roots on the 28th of the same month, both receiving excellent reviews. I'm Talking about Jerusalem was to open on the 27th of July. A week before that opening the Royal Court gave a party for the casts of Ionesco's Rhinoceros, which had transferred to The Strand Theatre (now The Novello), and the Wesker Trilogy. It was held on the stage of the Royal Court and during the celebrations I was introduced to Laurence Olivier, who was appearing in Rhinoceros.

He was very kind, staying to chat with me for five minutes or so about first-night nerves, critics and so on, but I couldn't help noticing that, at times, his attention was elsewhere. When I followed his eye-line, I realised that it was Joan Plowright who was proving the distraction.

I'm Talking about Jerusalem was perhaps not as ecstatically received as the two previous plays, but it was still a success. And when the two so-called 'butchers', Milton Shulman and Bernard Levin, *both* gave me a good notice, I felt that at last I was 'on my way'.

When the run came to an end I was immediately offered a leading role in one of the Armchair Theatre television plays that Sydney Newman was producing for ABC Television down at Teddington

Studios. Others were to follow in quick succession and, at long last, I was earning enough money to be able to move out of my parents' flat and find a place of my own. Living at home had been a godsend when money was scarce, but it had hampered my social life and severely restricted my sex life. Now, all that was about to change.

CHAPTER 12

DR WHO AND
THE ROYAL SHAKESPEARE COMPANY

When I started looking around for somewhere to live, I deliberately chose the Marylebone area of London, mainly because of my early-morning excursions there as a child in the Thirties, to buy stale bread. I don't know what, if anything, I was trying to prove. That I had come a long way since those days? Perhaps. Anyway, I found an unfurnished bijou flat in Thayer Street which I rented for £20 a month. I bought myself some furniture, had a phone installed (acquiring one of the sought-after Hunter prefixes) and settled down to enjoy the fruits of my success and new-found freedom.

In November 1961 I was asked to do a play at the Belgrade theatre in Coventry. It was called End of Conflict, had been written by Barry England, and was to be a world premiere. Sadly, it wasn't the big success that everyone had hoped for, and after six weeks I returned to London. While I was there I shared a dressing room with a young actor named Ian McKellen, who was one of the resident cast. Nice lad, I often wonder what became of him?

It was early in 1962 that I got my first part in a film. It was a prisoner-of-war film called The Password is Courage, directed by an eccentric American named Andrew Stone, and starring Dirk Bogarde. I didn't have a great deal to do, but I was around somewhere in almost every scene – and it was quite well paid. It was on this film that I learned an important lesson about film acting.

One day I was watching a scene where, in close-up, Dirk Bogarde had to convey the anger and despair of a man who had spent three years planning an escape, only to see it on the brink of discovery because of the stupidity of two escapees, one of them being me. From where I was standing he *appeared* to be doing nothing, but when I saw the rushes the following day it was all there – in his face and in his eyes. I had learned the first principle of film acting. When in close-up don't act – *think*. If you get it right the camera will do the rest. All the great film actors have this ability, to convey their innermost thoughts without the use of dialogue.

The film was shot almost entirely on location at a disused army camp somewhere near Epping. It was winter and conditions were fairly primitive for us 'POWs'. The old latrines had been pressed into service, and our meals were served in the cavernous, draughty mess hall on long tables with wooden benches. Being the star, Dirk Bogarde had his own Winnebego, but apart from that there was never any 'star' behaviour from him. There must have been a nucleus of about 15 actors in the cast I suppose, the rest being extras, but he knew us all by name, and every day, on a rotational basis, two of us would have lunch in his caravan with him and his long-time partner and manager, Anthony Forwood. About six months later I was at Pinewood Studios seeing somebody about a part in a film.

After the interview I went into the bar for a drink, and Dirk Bogarde was there with a couple of people. When he saw me he beckoned me over, shook my hand, and introduced me to his companions saying: "Mark and I worked on a film together a while back." In a profession where over-inflated egos abound, he was unpretentious, good at his job, and charming with it. He is sadly missed by all who knew him or worked with him.

It was in the autumn of 1963 that I was asked to go along to BBC Television Centre at White City to talk to Waris Hussein and Verity Lambert about the part of Marco Polo in an upcoming seven-episode story of Dr Who.

Dr Who started out as a children's programme but had soon begun reaching a much wider audience, attracting viewing figures in the region of 12 million. I had read one of the scripts by John Lucarotti and had liked it, and had got on well with both Waris Hussein, the director, and Verity Lambert, the producer. So I was rather pleased when I was offered the part. The money was nothing to write home about, but then it never was at the BBC. But I was to have all my costumes made for me, which made me eager to get started.

Looking back, I think Dr Who was probably one of the most enjoyable things I ever did. Waris was a delight to work with. He was charming, funny, imaginative and brilliant at his job. The resident cast were friendly and welcoming. And William Hartnell as the eponymous Dr Who was excellent. To my mind Bill Hartnell was one of the two best Dr Whos of all time because he had the right blend of eccentricity, irritability and unworldliness that the character needs. (In case you're wondering my other favourite Dr Who was Tom Baker). Bill could be a bit grumpy at rehearsals sometimes, though he always regretted it. I remember, after one day when he had been particularly tetchy he came into rehearsals next morning with a posy for each of the three ladies – and a large tin of biscuits for the rest of the cast.

Enjoyable as it was to be Marco Polo in Dr Who, none of us I'm sure ever expected it to be the cult classic it has become. I think part of the explanation for this is due to the fact that not long after it was transmitted the video tapes of the whole seven episodes were wiped clean, and no-one seems to know for certain how it happened. One theory is that it was some freak accident, but I think the reason is more mundane. It was done to save money. Back in the 1960s video tape was very expensive, but the tapes were re-usable. My guess is that somebody at the BBC needed some video tapes and went along to the Recorded Programmes Library, or wherever they kept used tapes, grabbed the first cassettes he could find, put them in the machine and wiped them clean. Unfortunately they just happened to be the tapes of Marco Polo.

There were no home video recorders back then. The only way you could record a TV programme was to place a cine-camera in front of the screen. The results were not very good quality, but lots of people did it, so the hope is, albeit a forlorn one, that one day somebody will find some dusty old reels of film in an attic somewhere, and it will be the long-lost Dr Who story of Marco Polo.

A few months later I was offered another film. For the past two years my friend Tom Bell had been making quite a name for himself, and had landed his first leading role in a major film; it was The L-Shaped Room, produced by Richard Attenborough, directed by Bryan Forbes, and starring Leslie Caron. I was offered a small part in it, one scene with Leslie Caron, but I was more than happy to accept.

One day during filming I had lunch with Leslie Caron, during which she asked me why I had never joined the Royal Shakespeare Company, and seemed surprised when I told her that I had never been invited to do so. Some weeks later I was asked to go along to the Aldwych Theatre to meet Peter Hall and Colin Graham, and do a reading for them. The upshot of that meeting was that I was offered the part of Edward Sterne in the John Whiting play *A Penny for a Song*. It was to be a big, prestige production for the RSC with a star-studded cast that included Judi Dench, Gwen Ffrangcon-Davies, Marius Goring, James Bree, Hugh Morton, Michael Gwynne, Newton Blick, Colin Jeavons and Henry Woolfe.

I had been 'in love' with Judi Dench since I had seen her in Franco Zefferelli's Romeo and Juliet at the Old Vic. Now I was working with her, and most of my scenes were with her. So it was inevitable, I suppose, that I fell in love with her; this time for real. Sadly, my love was unrequited. Judi, gently but firmly, kept me at arm's length. Try as I might, it was all to no avail; and although my ardour remained unquenched, I knew a lost cause when I saw one and finally, reluctantly, gave up the pursuit. Although Judi was a joy to work with, she was also a renowned practical joker, and it was at the sparsely-attended matinees that you had to be on your guard.

The main action of A Penny for a Song takes place in the cliff-top garden of a manor house on the Kent coast in the early 19th century, and my first entrance was at the beginning of the play. With a young boy in tow, I enter the garden where Judi is sitting and ask her for something to eat and drink, which she goes off to get. At one matinee she arrived back with a tray on which, instead of the usual tankard of ale and some bread and cheese, there was a tankard of foaming Andrew's Liver Salts, two lumps of rock hard breads and a piece of yellow sponge!

It was at another matinee that Noel Coward came to see the play, sitting in the front row among a group of elderly ladies. Apparently he would come over from Jamaica, where he lived as a tax exile, for the three months he was allowed to spend in Britain and see every play, musical, revue, opera and ballet in London. He came round after the show to see everybody and to say how much he had enjoyed it. I was sharing a dressing room with James Bree at the time, and it was there, for a few minutes, that I met and talked to the great Noel Coward.

We opened on the 1st of August 1962 to a cry of delight from most of the critics and a few sniffy ones, but overall it was a huge success. During the run the prolific British film-makers Roy and John Boulting came to a matinee, came backstage afterwards, and offered me a part in a film they were about to make called Heavens Above, starring Peter Sellers and featuring almost every comedy name in the business. It actually started shooting while the play was still on, which meant that, for a while, I was filming during the day and going straight to the theatre at night. Not something I would recommend, but it didn't really bother me. I was too busy enjoying myself.

One night my parents came to see the play; dad in his best Sunday suit and mum in a new coat and hat bought specially for the occasion. Afterwards I took them to the famous Rules restaurant in Maiden Lane for supper.

My dear father, being the shy, self-effacing man he was, was so over-awed by the opulence of the surroundings that he hardly ate any of the food he had ordered. On the other hand my mother tucked into everything with great relish and when we had all finished, she scraped all the leftovers onto one plate and stacked the other plates neatly underneath each other to: "Make it easier for the waiter when he came to clear the table."

As the run of A Penny for a Song was coming to an end Peter Hall invited me to join the RSC. It was an offer not afforded to many young actors, and I was flattered to be asked. Without wishing to appear conceited, I had been half expecting this might happen and had already weighed up the pros and cons, and had decided not to accept. With the benefit of hindsight it was probably a wrong decision, but those were heady times for me. Film and Television parts were coming my way on a fairly regular basis, bringing with them considerable sums of money. The pay at the RSC was just £20 a week – for everybody. Just by doing 'Heavens Above' I had earned the equivalent of almost three year's salary at the RSC! I know I shouldn't have let that influence me, but it did. At that point in my career I saw my immediate future in films and TV, not in the theatre. I thought that could come later. To be honest, there was another reason. I am basically a lazy person, and the theatre is hard work for very little financial reward; the recompense being the sense of achievement one feels that only working on a stage can bring.

I take consolation in the fact that there is little point in regretting the decision I made at that time (although I do) because if I were put back in that same position, *at that same time*, I would do exactly the same thing again.

CHAPTER 13

ONWARDS AND UPWARDS

In May 1963 I moved out of my flat in Thayer Street and rented a flat in Bloomsbury. Again, I suppose it was harking back to my youth, because it was there that I had trudged the streets as a reluctant telegram boy, and had often delivered telegrams to the very apartment block I was now living in. 1963 was also the year I was able to repay my dear parents for all the sacrifices they had made on my behalf over the past five years. For most of his life my father had cherished the hope that one day he and mum would make the pilgrimage to Lourdes, but at the ages of 63 and 60 respectively, that dream was beginning to look less and less likely.

Unknown to them, I contacted a Catholic tour agency who came up with the perfect package deal: a small conducted tour, with a priest as their guide. It began with a four-night stay at Lourdes, including a visit to Saint Bernadette's birthplace. Then on to Italy to visit Saint Francis of Assisi's birthplace, followed by a week in Rome, culminating in a grand tour of the Vatican and an audience with Pope John XX11. For my parents it was, quite literally, the journey of a lifetime. Apart from my father going to Germany with the army of occupation after the First World War, they both had never been further afield than Bournemouth in their entire lives. So you can imagine their excitement (not to say apprehension) as we saw them off at Victoria Station on the first leg of their journey to Dover.

Sadly, while they were on their tour, Pope John died suddenly. So although they were to be denied their eagerly anticipated audience, they had the unique experience of being able to pay their last respects to a Pope lying in state in the Vatican. On their return Chas, Kath and I gave them a small welcome-home party, after which they recounted, in awed tones, the wonders they had seen, the people

they had met, and the spiritual exaltation they had experienced throughout their journey.

When they had finished there was silence for a moment, then my father said: "Mind you, we didn't have one decent cup of tea all the time we were away."

In the early summer of 1963 Fred and Nellie, Joan's parents, decided to end their self-imposed exile in the wasteland of Luton and return to Ramsgate, where Fred opened a jellied eel and seafood shop. But after spending most of the summer ladling out jellied eels, or standing on her dad's cockle and whelk stall on the sea front, Joan decided to leave Ramsgate and find work in London. After talking it over with her parents, Fred and Nellie offered to look after David from Monday to Friday, with Joan coming back to be with him every weekend. David was six years old by now, attending a school just ten minutes walk away and doing well. He loved his grandparents, and they him, so perhaps the separation wasn't quite as painful and disruptive for him as it sounds. Even so, Joan was racked with misgivings when the time came for her to leave.

I had been going down to see David on a fairly regular basis, but, I have to say, not as often as I could, and should, have done. The reason was pure selfishness on my part. I was having the time of my life, making up for all the years of adversity and deprivation. In other words, I was too intent on having a good time to spend more time with my son. That same year I was offered another part in a major film. Having already worked for Bryan Forbes and Richard Attenborough, I was asked to be in their next production, *Seance on a Wet Afternoon*, again to be directed by Bryan Forbes and produced by Richard Attenborough, who was also co-starring with the American actress, Kim Stanley. It was a good part in an excellent film, which has since become a cult film classic. In America Kim Stanley won Best

Actress Award from the New York Film Critics Circle, and was nominated for an Oscar, while in England Richard Attenborough won the BAFTA Award for best actor.

It was during the filming of *Seance on a Wet Afternoon* that Bryan Forbes advised me to get my teeth fixed. When I was growing up, back in the 1930's, dentistry hadn't progressed very far from the Victorian era and orthodontics, such as they were, were only available to those who could afford to pay. So, for the want of a dental brace, my front teeth had grown slightly crooked. In real life and on stage this defect wasn't very noticeable, but in close-up on a 30 foot wide cinema screen there was definitely room for improvement. At this point in my career, with film work coming in on a fairly regular basis, I decided to take Bryan's advice, and had my four front teeth 'crowned'. As I recall it cost me somewhere in the region of £250, a small fortune to me at the time, but money I considered well spent as I now had a new, perfectly straight set of porcelain. What I hadn't bargained for, and what my dentist had omitted to tell me, was that after a year or so of wear and tear dental crowns are liable to work loose, and sometimes drop out! And thereby hangs another cautionary tale. Around 18 months later, for some now unaccountable reason, I agreed to do a two-hander play called *Two for the See-Saw* at the Civic Theatre, Scunthorpe. Why I accepted such an unappealing offer I cannot now recall. Scunthorpe is not a place anybody would want to go to voluntarily. The part wasn't something I'd always wanted to play, and the pay was Equity minimum! I can only assume that it might have been a touch of what actors call 'getting back to your roots'; i.e films and TV are all very well, but the *real* test for any actor is stepping out onto a stage in front of a live audience, knowing that for the next couple of hours you have to engage, stimulate and entertain perhaps 600 people, half of whom appear to have bronchitis.

But I think a more likely explanation is that it was only a four week engagement (one week's rehearsal and three weeks playing) so I probably thought, why not? My co-star was a charming young actress called Geraldine Hart. We worked well together during rehearsals in London, and arrived in Scunthorpe well prepared for the task ahead. However...during the action of the play, just before the end of the first act, Geraldine had to smack my face. Now, there is a way of doing a slap on stage that looks (and sounds) good but doesn't really hurt that much. This is done by *always keeping your wrist flexible as you deliver the slap*, something Geraldine understood in theory but seemed unable to achieve in practice. Consequently, every night I found myself on the receiving end of a teeth-rattling, head-jerking right hander. She would always apologise afterwards and promise to do better next time, but all to no avail.

Then one night disaster struck. As Geraldine's rigid right hand once again connected forcibly with the side of my face one of the dental crowns flew out of my mouth on an arcing trajectory, and dropped onto the apron of the stage just beyond the curtain line. As the curtain slowly descended to end act one I kept a frantic eye on where my tooth had landed, and as soon as the curtain touched the floor I was down on my hands and knees scrabbling around underneath it, desperately trying to retrieve my front tooth, so that I could get through the second act of a romantic comedy without looking like one of the village yokels in a comic opera.

Blissfully unaware of the mayhem she had caused, a bewildered Geraldine tentatively asked me what I was doing. "You knocked my bloody tooth out," I hissed through the gap in my gritted teeth, still blindly groping around under the curtain. By now, one by one, a small group of curious backstage staff had gathered behind my spread-eagled body, talking quietly among themselves. "What's going on?" "Geraldine knocked Mark's tooth out." "Why is he lying on the floor?" "He's looking for his tooth." "Oh!" Then, against all the odds, *I found my missing tooth*, and scrambled to my feet shouting: "Someone get me some chewing gum," as I hurried to my dressing room. Ten minutes later, with my front tooth stuck on with a wad of Wrigley's Spearmint; I managed to stagger through a seemingly interminable second act. The next day an obliging dentist re-cemented my front tooth back in and the play continued; needless to say, *without* the slap! Three weeks later, as the train taking me back to London pulled out of the station, I noticed that someone had blacked out the 'S' and the 'horpe' on one of the platform's Scunthorpe signs!

CHAPTER 14

DOROTHY SQUIRES
AND DOCTOR ZHIVAGO

In the spring of 1963 I was offered my first starring role in a television series for the BBC, called 'Catch Hand'. There were to be eight episodes, concerning two men (the Catch Hands of the title) who travelled the country taking on difficult or dangerous jobs other workers refused to accept, and my co-star was to be Anthony Booth. I had first met Tony Booth when he was sharing a flat with Tom Bell, and I hadn't exactly warmed to him. Now we were to be working together. After a few days of warily weighing each other up we found that we quite liked one another, and went on to become firm friends.

It was while I was filming Catch Hand that I first met Dorothy Squires. She happened to drop by the house of a mutual friend while I was visiting, and before she left had invited me to one of her famous parties at her home in Bexley, Kent. The bash was - as all Dot's parties were - a star-studded affair, packed with well-known names from the music and variety side of show business. I still can't remember exactly how she and I ended up in bed together that night, but we did, and a bizarre kind of relationship began. From the start it was an unlikely liaison. Dot was 18 years older than me, and not the kind of woman I normally found attractive. She was loud and brash, wore chunky, ostentatious jewellery, drove a Ford Thunderbird, and swore like a Billingsgate porter.

She had been devastated by the break up of her marriage to Roger Moore, and was pretty cynical as far as men were concerned, but we seemed to hit it off, in a macabre kind of way. To describe our subsequent affair as 'tempestuous' would be an understatement. We both had explosive tempers allied to short fuses, and we had constant, pyrotechnical rows. But the biggest mistake we made was going on holiday together.

When I had finished filming Catch Hand, Dot, myself, Ernie Dunstall who was Dot's accompanist, and two of Dot's gay friends, Adrian and Bobby, went to Torremolinos on the Costa del Sol, where we had rented a large villa. Things started to go wrong almost as soon as we arrived. The main bone of contention being Dot's penchant for sitting on the beach all day, every day. I have never been a sun worshipper and I can't swim, so sitting on a crowded beach all day with sun block smeared all over my body and sand in my crotch held very little appeal. In fact none at all.

Consequently, while Dot lay prostrate on the beach I would go into Torremolinos, where you could buy the previous day's English newspaper, find a shady bar and partake of some tapas and a glass or two of rioja. I was soon to be joined by Ernie Dunstall who, like me, couldn't see the point of trailing down to the beach and spending the entire day in a state of total inertia. Consequently we decided to hire a car for a week and drive out to somewhere different every day. On the first day we bought a map and, with Ernie driving, motored over to Granada and spent an enjoyable day exploring the city. On another day we went to Toledo. Some days we would just drive and if we saw something that looked interesting we would stop and explore it. Another day we went to Malaga Airport and took the short-hop 'plane over to Casablanca. Even at night there was disagreement. Dot, Adrian and Bobby usually wanted to go to a club, while Ernie and I favoured a quiet restaurant where you could actually hear what everyone was saying. The sense of relief when we finally landed at Heathrow was almost palpable. Each one of us, I'm sure, making a mental note never to go on holiday with certain people ever again.

Catch Hand was transmitted during the summer of 1964, and although it regularly attracted audiences of six to seven million viewers a week the BBC decided against commissioning another series, and it was dropped. In the early autumn of 1964 Maggie

Cartier cast me as 'Engineer at the Dam' in the film *Doctor Zhivago*. However, this didn't mean I had definitely secured the part. Apparently, two other actors had previously been cast in the role and sent out to Spain, only to be sent back by director David Lean as 'unsuitable'. It was only two scenes, a fairly long dualogue at the beginning of the film, and a shorter one at the end, both with Alec Guinness! So it was with some trepidation that I flew out from Heathrow to Madrid.

I was met off the 'plane, by a middle-aged Spanish man in an ill-fitting suit who fast-tracked me through customs and passport control, and then drove me to the Hilton Hotel. After he had gone I thought perhaps I ought to have tipped him for his trouble, but I'm rather glad I didn't. I found out later that he was somebody quite high up in Spanish Customs, who had been assigned to the film to facilitate the many comings and goings at Madrid airport of people connected to *Doctor Zhivago*. After hanging around for a couple of days I was taken out to the location to be approved (or otherwise) by David Lean. On the outskirts of Madrid they had built a complete Russian street about a hundred metres long, with shops, restaurants, etc, and a working replica of a Russian tram (circa 1905) with hundreds of Spanish extras in period costume milling around. It was all, so I was told, for one long tracking shot featuring Omar Sharif and Julie Christie.

During a break in the shooting I was taken over to meet David Lean. I was introduced and we shook hands. He studied me for a moment with his icy-blue eyes, smiled and said: "Fine." I had made it! A day or two later I was introduced to Sir Alec Guinness. As we shook hands the first thing he said to me was: "Please, call me Alec." In manner and bearing he reminded me a little of John LeMesurier, he was shy, softly spoken, courteous and utterly charming.

The only other actors staying at the Hilton were Rita Tushingham and Tom Courteney. I had met Tom Courtney briefly before, and before long we had palled-up, and began hitting a few nightspots together. One day Alec asked Tom Courteney and I if we would care to accompany him to an exhibition of Spanish Zapateado.

It was being performed by some famous Spanish dancers and which, we were told, was the *real* thing – none of your tourist rubbish, this was strictly for *aficionados,* so we went along. It was a small venue holding about a hundred people I suppose, and it was packed. There were two wonderful flamenco guitarists, who also sang, and the dancers were brilliant; but after a while, to our untutored eyes, it all became rather repetitious. One couple would finish their spot and sit down, and another couple would stand up and do (it seemed to us) the same spins, stamps and heel-taps that the previous pair had done; apparently to the same musical accompaniment. It wasn't, of course. There are many subtle variations and nuances in the movements and steps in Zapateado which we, being *extranjeros,* didn't appreciate. Anyway, it was this that Tom and I began discussing, sotto voce, while the dancing was in progress. During a short break a man approached us and, speaking English, and politely informed us that if we wished to have a conversation, would we please have the good manners to wait until the dancing was over. Suitably chastened, we sat through the second part in silence. Afterwards we both apologised to Alec who, I could see, had been embarrassed by the incident. He shrugged it off, smiled that shy smile, and said: "The Spanish do take their flamenco rather seriously, I'm afraid."

About three weeks after my arrival in Madrid, the whole film unit moved down to Salamanca near the border with Portugal to shoot all the dam scenes at the huge Aldeadavila dam. It was here that Alec and I were to do our scenes in the Engineer's office. So there was just Alec, Rita Tushingham and me, each ensconced in a large, luxury caravan. One morning we were waiting to do a shot of Alec and me, standing at my office window, looking down on the hundreds of workers, men and women, arriving to work at the dam. It was a blazingly hot day; and while we were sitting comfortably in the shade being supplied with cooling drinks, there were two or three hundred Spanish extras, dressed as Russian peasants, standing in the blistering sun, waiting to do shots of them entering the dam.

They were being paid just £3 a day plus food; which wasn't a great deal of money even in 1964, but apparently there had been no shortage of applicants for the job. As we were sitting chatting, Alec suddenly got up and went over to a crowd of extras directly in front of us, spoke to a heavily pregnant woman, brought her back to where we were sitting in the shade, set her down in his own chair, then turned to an assistant and said: "Would you mind bringing me a chair?" Then adding: "And a cold drink for the lady." She sat with us for about 20 minutes I suppose, obviously greatly relieved to be sitting down and out of the sun, but a little tense and self-conscious. When at last the call to 'Stand by' came, Alec stood up, helped her out of her chair, and watched as she joined the other extras and, with a little wave, move off.

When Doctor Zhivago was released in 1965, the scene I had with Alec Guinness at the end of the film had been cut, leaving me with just the one scene. Not that it bothered me that much. I had worked with, and briefly got to know, one of the all-time great actors, and that was reward enough. Tucked away among my most treasured souvenirs is an envelope containing two tickets for a bullfight at the Las Ventas bullring in Madrid, and a hand-written note on one of his cards from Alec Guinness, apologising for not being able to accompany me to the *corrida* (which he had arranged) telling me to dispose of the tickets as I saw fit, and signed simply 'Alec'. When Alec Guinness died in 2000 at the age of 86, we lost one of the last of the gentlemen actors.

When I returned to London I was not out of work for very long. Once again fortune was my friend and I was provided with yet another example of how luck plays such a crucial role in the uncertain life of an actor. An American director named Philip Wiseman had arrived in town to cast the London production of Tennessee Williams' Night of the Iguana. Sian Phillips had already accepted the leading female role and he was looking for someone to play the part of T. Lawrence Shannon, the male lead. One night he happened to have the TV on in his hotel room and saw me in one of the final episodes of Catch Hand. He made a note of my name, and rang my agent the following day.

Subsequently, I went along to see him at the Savoy Hotel, had a chat, read two or three speeches from the play, and was offered the part! It was the biggest breakthrough in my career; and it had come about by a stroke of unimaginable good luck. It was during rehearsals of the play that I fell in love again. As the weeks went by I found myself more and more attracted to a young actress named Patricia Shakesby. She had golden red hair, a wonderful figure, and an exquisitely beautiful face, and I was smitten. By now I had the sense to know that if I went in all guns blazing, I would ruin everything, so I decided to bide my time.

A couple of weeks before we opened, Sian Phillips invited me to dinner at her home in Heath Street in Hampstead where she lived with her then husband Peter O'Toole. It was a jolly evening with the wine flowing – and being consumed – in copious quantities. As the evening wore on the other guests gradually all staggered off into the night, and Sian went to bed, leaving Peter and I to keep the flag flying. From then on things began to go downhill rather quickly. Peter started pouring alarmingly large brandies, and like a fool I tried to match him drink for drink. It was to be my undoing. When I finally lurched to my feet to leave, I fell flat on my face and passed out.

The next thing I remember is finding myself being carried upstairs by Peter, who had me over his shoulder in a fireman's lift.
How he was still able to *climb* the stairs was a miracle, never mind carrying a 175 pound drunken actor on his back. Peter was working on a film at the time, and even in my drink-befuddled state it did occur to me that just one small stumble and a major movie and a West End opening would be in jeopardy. Fortunately, he negotiated the stairs safely, dumped me unceremoniously onto a bed, and left me to sleep it off. How I got up, and got through, the following morning I'll never know. I had a hangover of such monumental proportions it was more like a flyover!

We were rehearsing in a room above a pub in Swiss Cottage and Peter was there waiting for me at lunch time with a glass of what looked like muddy water. "It's my own remedy," he said, handing me the glass. "Great for hangovers – if you can keep it down." It tasted absolutely vile, but it did the trick and I was able to get through the rest of the day...just.

On February 24th 1965 we played two weeks at the New Pembroke theatre in Croydon, followed by two more weeks at the Hippodrome Golders Green, before coming to the Savoy Theatre in the Strand at the end of March. The opening of the play promised to be a grand occasion. Tennessee Williams had come over from America for the first night, and a reception had been laid on at the Savoy Hotel after the show. For the past four weeks I had been consolidating my friendship with the fair Patricia, and had decided to ask her out for the first time during the after-show party. To this end I told Dot that only cast members had been invited to the reception afterwards. Her immediate reaction was: "If I can't come to the party, I'm not coming to the first night," which was fine by me. During the first interval of the play the stage door keeper brought me up a note, it was from Dot and went something like this: "Have arranged our own party at Joe Allen's after the show. I will await your arrival." I ignored it.

The first night was a triumph. A packed house gave us a rapturous reception, none more so than Tennessee Williams who leaped from his seat in the front row roaring his approval.

After a few glasses of champagne in my dressing room I slipped on my newly acquired midnight blue dinner jacket, and went along to the party at the Savoy Hotel. As soon as I arrived Tennessee Williams came up to me, shook my hand, and told me I was: "The best T. Lawrence Shannon of them all." It was an enormous compliment, considering the part had been played on Broadway by Patrick O'Neal, and by Richard Burton in the film. However, Mr Williams had been drinking rather heavily for most of the evening, which might, perhaps, have impaired his critical faculties a little. All the same, it was a great honour, coming from one of the greatest living playwrights and a double Pulitzer Prize winner.

From then on I spent most of the time talking to the lovely

Patricia. She had given me a first-night present of a book of poetry, and I sensed that, at last, my affections were being returned. I took Patricia out to dinner several times after that, always returning her to her home in Bayswater afterwards. Then, on Easter Sunday, we had a meal together, went back to my apartment, Patricia stayed the night, and love blossomed.

The big problem I had now was how to tell Dot. Ours had never been the greatest love story ever told, but I felt I ought to tell her it was over. Dot reacted to the bad news the way she always reacted to bad news. She went berserk. I kept trying to explain the situation to her over the phone, but I couldn't get a word in edgeways, sideways, vertically or horizontally. For the next two weeks my phone rang incessantly, and I was forced to take it off the hook at night to get some sleep. Eventually things began to cool down a little. The constant phone calls stopped, and Dot seemed to adopt a more conciliatory attitude when I talked to her. So when she rang me late one night from a recording studio in south London where she had just finished recording a new album, and invited me over for a celebratory drink for old time's sake I thought, 'Why not?' After a pleasant chat and couple of glasses of champagne, Dot offered to drop me off at my flat. Alarm bells should have started ringing right then but, trusting soul that I am, they didn't. As soon as the car began to move Dot locked all the doors and said: "Right, you bastard. Now I'm taking *you* for a ride," and so saying put her foot down on the accelerator.

Now the Ford Thunderbird is a *very* powerful car, and we went from nought to 80 in about ten seconds flat. Fortunately, it was around two o'clock in the morning and there was very little traffic around as we scorched a fiery trail across south London, jumping red lights and rounding corners on two wheels. I tried reasoning with her, but Dot wasn't listening as she sat, grim faced and silent, behind the steering wheel. The really frightening thing was that Dot wasn't a very good driver at the best of times, and this was not the best of times. I kept hoping that a police car would get on our tail and bring our roller-coaster ride to an end. But, as we all know, there's never a policeman around when you really need one, and we careered wildly through New Cross untroubled by the boys in blue.

As we left the Metropolitan Police area and entered into Kent County Constabulary country, it seemed even more unlikely to me that we would be brought to a halt, except by the intervention of a brick wall, or a tree.

Down winding country lanes we skidded, Monaco Rally style, until suddenly the car screeched to a whiplash-inducing halt. "This is where you get off," Dot said grimly. I got out and Dot drove away, leaving me in the middle of nowhere. I had to walk about half a mile before I spotted a telephone box, from where I called a taxi to take me home. To paraphrase Congreve: "Heaven has no rage, like love to hatred turned. Nor Hell no fury like Dot Squires scorned"

During the time we were together Dorothy Squires and I, along with Ernie Dunstall, wrote five songs – two of which were recorded by Dot and three by The Bachelors, a hugely popular singing trio of the time. We also collaborated in writing a musical about Charles II and Nell Gwynne, entitled 'Old Rowley'. It took us about six months to write and when it was finished Dot hired a recording studio and with me narrating, Ernie on a synthesizer, Dot singing all Nell Gwynne's songs and the Mike Samme's Singers doing the others, we put it all on disc.

Sadly in spite of Dot's Herculean efforts to 'sell' it (somebody once said that if Dot Squires wants to sell you something she doesn't knock on your door – she kicks it in!) we couldn't find any backers. And Old Rowley was never produced. The sting of rejection was felt far more deeply by Dot than by Ernie or me. It had been her conception, her baby, and nobody wanted it. Dot never gave up on Old Rowley. Long after Ernie and I had moved on she took every opportunity she could to plug it – all to no avail.

One last story about Dorothy Squires. It was Christmas time and Ken Parry was playing Dame in Mother Goose at Palmers Green in north London and Dot decided to go and see it. She arrived, having had a drink or two en route, wearing a full-length mink coat and, with her entourage trailing behind her, settled noisily in the front row.

Now there is a tradition in pantomime that if someone you know is in the audience, you somehow contrive to mention their name. As the curtain rose on the second act Kenny was seated centre stage shelling peas. "Dear me," he said: "Nobody loves me, nobody loves me. Thank goodness I'll always be welcome at Dorothy Squires' house." From the front row of the stalls Dot was heard to say loudly: "Not after this fucking performance you won't!" Their friendship was never quite the same after that.

To be fair to Dot – she adored my son David; often having him to stay weekends at her house in Bexley. When he was eleven years old she took him with her on a short tour, bringing him on stage every night to sing 'You're my best Beau' from the musical Auntie Mame, in a duet with her which invariably brought the house down. Dorothy Squires died in 1998 at the age of 83, homeless and penniless. It was a tragic end to what had been a long – and at one time – hugely successful career. When I heard of Dot's passing I telephoned Ernie Dunstall (Dot's pianist and arranger) and he gave me the date, the time and place of her burial. I wrote it all down and, on the appointed day, my son David and I took a mini-cab to a cemetery in Streatham, SW London, arriving about fifteen minutes before the cortege was expected. After hanging around for about half an hour we began to suspect that something was amiss, made some enquiries – and realised we had come to the wrong cemetery, which meant we had missed Dot's funeral, which had been at Streatham *Vale* cemetery!

Over a drink in a nearby pub I said to David 'How could I have made such a stupid mistake?' David shrugged and said 'Dot didn't want us there.' I read recently that Welsh Heritage were going to put up a blue plaque on the council house in Dafen, Carmarthenshire where Dot lived as a child, paid for by (now) Sir Roger Moore.

CHAPTER 15

MY BIG BREAK!

By 1965 Joan had been living and working in London for almost two years, and we had been meeting up from time to time for a meal or a drink. In 1964 she had taken a job as a wine waitress at the Establishment Club in Greek Street; and it was there that she had met the lovely John LeMesurier.

John's marriage to Hattie Jacques had broken up some time before, and after a year-long courtship (John was rather old fashioned that way) they were now living together at an apartment in Baron's Court. They both came to see me in the show one night, and over dinner afterwards Joan told me that she and John were planning to marry, and that she was already in the process of divorcing me on the grounds of desertion. On the same day, in the same court, Hattie was divorcing John for adultery, naming Joan as co-respondent.

It was all very civilised and completely amicable, with just a hint of collusion between the two ladies involved, who just happened to be the best of friends. A few weeks later a photograph of Joan, standing outside the Divorce Courts, appeared on the front page of the Evening Standard. The caption above the picture read: "The other woman." It was June 1965, and I was a single man again. By the summer of 1966 Joan and John had only been married for six month when something happened that was to completely change their lives. One night John brought Tony Hancock back to their apartment for dinner, and by the time the evening had ended Joan and Tony had fallen hopelessly in love with each other, and were about to embark on a tempestuous two-year affair.

At that time Tony Hancock was a huge star, with his television comedy show Hancock's Half-Hour regularly attracting audiences of

20 million or more. However, there was one big obstacle in their relationship; Tony was an alcoholic. Apparently when sober he could be charming, funny and considerate, but once the drink had been taken he could become, in Joan's own words, 'a monster'. Consequently there were constant acrimonious break-ups, followed by a remorseful Tony tearfully begging Joan to come back, which she invariably did.

By 1968, after many highs and lows, dry-outs and aversion therapies, Tony had managed to stop drinking and had accepted an offer to go to Australia to work on a new comedy series. Before he left Joan promised to write to him every day while he was away and, if he remained sober for a year, to marry him. After Tony left, John, being the gentleman he was, invited Joan to stay at the apartment they had once shared, with her own separate bedroom. It was an offer Joan accepted. On the face of it, this seemed an odd arrangement but, as John was away a lot of the time, it worked well enough.

Then a train of events occurred which set in motion a despairing, downward spiral that would ultimately end in tragedy. In Britain, a nationwide postal strike was called, and any letters Joan had already posted were marooned in sealed up pillar boxes or deserted sorting offices. In Australia, Tony, having no knowledge of the postal strike paralysing Britain, became concerned when Joan's letters suddenly stopped. Then, as more days passed and no letters arrived he became more and more despondent which, in turn, started him drinking again.

As the strike dragged on, Joan tried desperately to telephone Tony to explain what had happened, but due to a combination of antiquated 1960s telecommunications technology and an overload on the system caused by the strike, she was never able to contact him. By now Tony was in deep despair. The TV series he was working on was not the success he had hoped it would be. He was drinking heavily and the woman he loved seemed to have deserted him.

In desperation, thinking Joan might possibly be with out son David in Ramsgate, he put in a call to her parents' home which was answered by Nellie, Joan's mother. Nellie harboured a deep dislike of Tony and gave him very short shrift. When Tony asked if Joan was there her reply went something like this: "She isn't here, she's with John. She has gone back to him and wants nothing more to do with you. You have caused enough damage in our family. She is happy now, so just leave her alone." Then she put the 'phone down on him.

It was not true of course, but for Tony it was the final blow. Some little while later he sat down and wrote one last, poignant letter to Joan, and then wrote: "Too many things seemed to go wrong," on a piece of paper and took an overdose of sleeping tablets. Around three or four o'clock in the morning of 25th June 1968 the telephone rang in the flat at Baron's Court, which John answered. It was a mutual friend ringing from Australia with the news of Tony's Hancock's suicide. Not quite sure what to do, John finally went into Joan's bedroom, gently woke her, and told her the sad news. At which Joan began to wail with grief and became inconsolable.

Now at a complete loss and unable to cope, John picked up the 'phone and called me. Apologising profusely, he explained the situation and asked if I would come over to the flat and try to pacify Joan, which I did. I sat by her bedside for the rest of the night holding her hand and comforting her until, from sheer emotional exhaustion, she fell into a deep sleep.

Once again, to give Dorothy Squires her due, as soon as she heard the news about Tony and how distraught Joan had become, she immediately invited Joan down to her house in Bexley. It was an offer Joan gratefully accepted. And it was there, with Dot's help, that Joan was able to come to terms with her untimely loss and pick up the scattered shards of her life.

Although the notices for Night of the Iguana had been good, after about three months the audiences began to dwindle, and at the beginning of July we were told that we were coming off. Shortly before we closed, an American Film director came backstage to see me after the show one night accompanied by Maud Spector, a well known casting director. His name was Michael O'Herlihey, and he had come to talk to me about a film he was to direct for the Walt Disney Corporation entitled *The Prince of Donegal,* a swashbuckling adventure story set in 17th century Ireland, but to be shot in England.

Peter McEnery was to play the eponymous prince, and they wanted to know if I would be interested in doing a screen test for the part of his rascally elder brother. I did the screen test, and after about a week they rang my agent to tell me I had got the part. The offer finally agreed was this: I would be paid a fee of £3,000 (a goodly sum at that time) I would have third billing – above the title. I would have all my costumes made for me by Nathan's of Drury Lane, and – this was the bit that had me turning cartwheels – on completion of the picture I would sign a three-year exclusive contract with the Walt Disney Corporation starting at £15,000 a year, and increasing by £5,000 each year after that.

This was *IT* - the big one! Everything I had been working for over the past seven years had at last come to fruition – in glorious Technicolor!!!

Knowing that the role would call for a certain amount of athleticism on my part I decided to get myself really fit. For the next six weeks I worked out for two or three hours every morning at the YMCA gymnasium in Great Russell Street. I took an intensive course of horse-riding lessons at a riding school in Barnet, and a crash course in sword fighting. I stopped drinking and cut down drastically on my smoking. By the time the first day of shooting arrived I was leaner and fitter that I had ever been in my life. The first two days of filming went well, but on the third day, literally out of the blue, disaster struck. It was a glorious autumn day and we were on location at Chobham Common in Surrey.

It was a straightforward action shot, me on foot, being chased by two men on horseback.

As I ran pell-mell down a steep hill towards my waiting horse I caught my foot in a hole, fell headlong, and with a crack as sharp as a pistol shot, broke my ankle. I was stretchered off the hillside, taken to the nearest hospital, and almost before the plaster around my ankle had set, had been replaced on the picture by the actor Tom Adams. So it was goodbye to a starring part in a movie, a trip to Hollywood and a lucrative three year contract, and hello to three months on crutches, six months out of work, and a small pile of ashes where all my hopes had once burned so brightly.

As one who by fate's fell hand had been so cruelly smote, I felt I'd had more than my share of misfortune, but the *coup de grace* was yet to come. I had assumed, not unreasonably, that as a matter of course some sort of financial compensation would be forthcoming to me, particularly from a company as wealthy as Walt Disney Inc. Especially since the accident had occurred while I was actually filming a scene in one of their movies. I had assumed wrongly. The Walt Disney Company made it crystal clear that they were prepared to pay me only for the three days I had worked, and not a penny more. I consulted my union, Equity, who in turn talked to their legal department.

They informed me that the only way I could sue the Disney Corporation for damages and loss of earnings was on the grounds of negligence, but advised strongly against it. For a start it could take up to two years for the case to come to Court. Secondly, there *had* been a stunt-double standing by who I could have called upon, had I thought the stunt too dangerous to do myself. In other words – I didn't have a leg to stand on, literally or metaphorically. Never having been blessed with an over-abundance of moral fibre, and facing a long period of enforced inactivity, I rapidly descended into a slough of self-pity and self-indulgence.

I began to drink heavily, seldom getting to bed before rosy-fingered dawn came a-tapping on the window pane. My drinking companions were Tom Bell and/or Tony Booth and more often than not we picked up a few more pieces of human flotsam as we ploughed the rough seas of bacchanalia. Our starting point was, invariably, The Salisbury, at that time an actor's pub in St. Martin's Lane, where we would foregather around the time of the noon-day gun. When that chucked out we would wend our way to The Kismet, a subterranean drinking club in nearby Gt. Newport Street, where we could booze the afternoon away in noisome discomfort. Ah, the dear old Kismet. It was four underground coal cellars knocked into one, and always permeated with the faint but unmistakable aroma of sewage. It was a haven for out-of-work actors, a place where they could meet their cronies, curse their luck, and drown their disappointments.

There is a story that one afternoon an actor called Dennis Shaw was entering the club with a young actor who had never been to the Kismet before. "What's that funny smell?" said the young actor as they came down the stairs. "That, dear boy," Dennis growled, "is the smell of failure." I must digress for a while to tell you a little about Dennis Shaw. Den-Den, as he was known, was short and squat with a face of Hogarthian proportions, covered with lumps and excrescences; earning him the unkind but apt soubriquet, 'The Warthog'. He borrowed money from *everybody* and never paid it back, and after a few drinks became even more aggressive and obnoxious than he was when sober. He knew the inside of every paddy-wagon and police cell in the West Central Division of the Metropolitan Police, and had been barred, at one time or another, from every pub, club, bar and restaurant within a three mile radius of Charing Cross.

But for all that, there was something likable about the old reprobate, and when he died there was a genuine feeling of sadness at the loss of a great 'character'. Because he had died, as he had lived, deeply in debt, a collection was raised by his fellow actors to give him a decent burial. On the day of his funeral as the cortege approached the gates of Highgate Cemetery somebody had hung a banner across the entrance; it read, 'DENNIS, YOU'RE BARRED!'

After about six months I was back on my feet again (literally) and TV parts were being offered to me on a regular basis, but somehow it wasn't the same. Something else had been broken along with my ankle, it was the momentum that had been building up before my accident, and I had a feeling it would never return in quite the same way again.

CHAPTER 16

JOHNNY MATHIS, MICHAEL WINNER AND PATRICK MCGOOHAN

In 1966 something happened that provided me with a story with which I have bored countless dinner parties ever since. Now it's your turn.

It was around one o'clock in the morning and I was preparing for an early night when the telephone rang. It was Tony Booth. He was at a swell party hosted by the singer Johnny Mathis and had arranged with the host for me to come and join them. In no time at all I was in a taxi on my way to the address in Knightsbridge that Tony had given me. When I arrived the party was still in full swing. Tony introduced me to Johnny Mathis and I had a great time. Johnny Mathis was a charming and gracious host, but with the dawn light already slanting across the greensward of Hyde Park, he declared the party over. There were only about half a dozen of us left, and one of our number asked Johnny Mathis if he would sing one last song before we went. His pianist having long since departed Johnny said (we were all on first name terms by now) he couldn't sing unaccompanied. Tony Booth immediately said: "Mark can play the piano." I tried to explain to Johnny that I only played by ear and that my playing wasn't all that good, but my protestations were brushed aside and I was led over to the white, baby grand. "Can you play Misty?" Johnny asked as I sat down. "What key do you sing it in?" I asked, nervously. "Whatever key you play it in, I'll sing it in," he replied, smiling. So, not taking any chances, I played it in the key of C.

Johnny Mathis sang it through, everybody clapped, Johnny patted me on the back, and then we all went home. And that's how I came to play the piano for Johnny Mathis. Not many people can say *that*!

In the summer of 1967 Michael Winner offered me a part in a film he was to direct called I'll Never Forget What's 'is Name, starring Oliver Reed, Carol White, and Orson Welles in a 'guest' role. It was the part of a private detective hired to follow the character Oliver Reed was playing, a smallish role but I accepted it because (a) I would be working with Oliver Reed, whom I admired as an actor, and (b) because all my scenes were to be filmed in the beautiful city of Cambridge (where, incidentally, Michael Winner had taken his MA (Hons) degree).

There is no sitting on the fence when it comes to Michael Winner, no messing about, you either like him - or you can't stand him! It has to be said that he is not the easiest man in the world to like (John LeMesurier once described him as 'unlovable') but I got on well with him, and he with me. I also got on well with Oliver Reed; which was just as well, because all my scenes were with him.

One of those scenes was Oliver Reed in a punt on the river Cam, with me – in the background – walking along the river-bank watching him. It was what is known as a 'reverse shot' from Carol White's point of view. Carol White was not in the punt, her place being taken by Michael Winner and the cameraman, both crouched at the other end of the punt with Michael speaking Carol's lines to Oliver Reed.

I was too far away to hear what was being said, but as I watched, to my amazement, Oliver Reed suddenly threw the pole into the water, stepped off the side of the punt, and started swimming towards the bank where I was standing. For a moment I thought it must be part of the action...until I heard angry shouts from Michael Winner, who was standing up in the punt and gesticulating so ferociously that he almost capsized the boat. Oliver Reed reached the bank, climbed out of the water, and calmly started to walk back to his hotel, leaving Michael Winner and the cameraman marooned in the middle of the Cam drifting helplessly down river. Michael has always maintained that Oliver Reed *fell* into the water – but I know better.

Over dinner that night Oliver Reed told me that Michael was driving him mad with his incessant talking. Finally Oliver said to him: "Michael, if you don't stop rabbiting, I'm going straight back to the hotel." Michael said: "How do you intend to do that, dear, in the middle of the Cam?"

Another time while out on location we had broken for lunch and, as it was a fine day, Michael Winner, Oliver Reed, myself and some of the crew were all sitting around outside in the sunshine eating our food when an elderly bag lady came along. "Wos goin' on 'ere?" she demanded to know. "We're making a film, love," said one of the crew. She eyed us suspiciously for a moment, then held out her hand and said: "How about helpin' me out with some money then?"

A glint of mischief flared in Oliver Reed's eye. "You see that man sitting over there," he said, pointing to Michael Winner who was sitting alone at a table, having given strict instructions that he was not to be disturbed. "He's the director of this film, *and* he's a millionaire. He'll give you some money."

We all watched with glee as the bag lady approached Michael, who, to our astonishment, invited her to sit down and was courteous and charming to the old lady. He chatted amiably with her for a few minutes before getting his secretary to give her some money. (Like royalty, Michael did not carry money on his person). Then, before she left, he arranged for the location caterers to pack some food in plastic containers for her to take away. Game, set and match: Winner!

In 2009 the National Film Theatre on the Left Bank was showing a selection of British films of the 1960s. One of them was I'll Never Forget What's 'is Name and Michael Winner was to be guest speaker, so I went along with two friends to watch the movie. After the screening Michael came on, talked about making the film and answered questions from the audience, then got up to leave. As I hadn't seen Michael for over 40 years I thought I'd go over and say 'Hello'. I went up to him and said: "Michael, I'm Mark Eden…" He immediately said: "I know who you are, Mark, and I'm very pleased to see you. You and I must be the only two left who worked on that picture. They've laid a reception for me with food and drink, why don't you come and join us?" When I told him I was with two friends, he said: "Bring them with you," which I did. I spent about 15 minutes talking to Michael and before I left he asked me to write down my address. Each year since then he has sent me a Christmas card.

But for all their differences on the film (and there were several other incidents) Michael was enormously fond of Oliver Reed; and the affection was mutual. When Oliver Reed died suddenly in 1999 Michael went over to Dublin for the funeral and delivered a moving tribute to the actor that he had written himself. In 1967 I was offered the part of Number 100 in an episode of The Prisoner entitled It's Your Funeral. Again, at the time I looked upon it as just another job. I had absolutely no idea that it would eventually become one of the biggest cult TV series ever.

Patrick McGoohan was the associate producer, writer and star. A strange, remote and taciturn man who never mixed, socially or otherwise, with any of the cast or crew, and who after every scene would go straight back to his dressing room and lock the door. A dressing room where (I was reliably informed by his dresser) there was a large crucifix on the wall! Apparently he also had special clauses written into his contracts that there would be no 'love interest' or 'love scenes'. When working with him I always felt that he was like an unexploded bomb, liable to blow up at any minute; and I wasn't far wrong.

On my third day on the set Patrick McGoohan was having a slight altercation with director Robert Asher when suddenly, in front of a packed studio, he blew his top. Shouting at the top of his voice he sacked the director, announced that he would take over direction himself, and stormed off back to his dressing room. Leaving behind a shocked and apprehensive cast and crew, none more concerned than me; I had a big fight scene with him scheduled for the very next day!

Being the 'Jack-the-lad' that I was at that time I had turned down the offer of a stunt-double, and was going to do the fight myself. Big mistake! When the time came, Patrick McGoohan, myself and the fight arranger painstakingly went through all the moves of the fight in 'slow-motion' so that we knew exactly what we were doing before the cameras rolled.

To my relief it all went well, right up to the point where McGoohan, having knocked me to the floor, leapt astride me and, with his hands round my throat, forces me to tell him where I had planted a bomb. When you are doing fight scenes of course all the blows are faked, and there is a way of putting your hands around someone's throat, which looks like you are strangling them without actually doing so.

But Mr McGoohan either didn't know of this technique or didn't care for it. As his hands tightened ominously around my throat I looked up into his wild-eyed, rage-contorted face and realised we had a problem. The arrangement was that after about a minute or two of dialogue I would tell him what he wanted to know, then throw him off me and slide down a slight slope where (in another shot) the Rover (the big balloon) would smother me. However, due to a constricted windpipe I was having great difficulty breathing, so I cut to the last line and, summoning all my rapidly waning strength, managed to throw him off me. McGoohan, ignoring the plan, *clung onto me* so that we both rolled, over and over down to the bottom of the incline, ending up with him landing on top of me – all 185 pounds of him! On the shout of 'Cut' McGoohan leapt to his feet, looked down at where I lay gasping for breath, nodded his head and walked off.

In stark contrast back in 1963 I had been in an episode of The Saint series entitled The Invisible Millionaire, starring Roger Moore. The atmosphere in the studio throughout my time there was relaxed and congenial. Roger Moore was charming and affable and, more importantly, was brilliant at doing fight scenes, which was just as well because once again I had opted to do the fight I had with him myself.

But to return to The Prisoner, when It's Your Funeral was transmitted the scene where I was killed by the big balloon had been omitted. So the next morning I rang the casting director Rose Tobias-Shaw to find out why. She told me that the producers had liked my character and had cut the scene in case they might want to use me again. It didn't happen!

From the beginning 1968 was a good year for me, work wise. In February I did a film called The Curse of the Crimson Altar, a horror movie with Christopher Lee and one of my boyhood heroes, a man who was literally a legend in his own lifetime, Boris Karloff. Boris was a charming, modest, courteous and amusing man and in the long waits between takes would regale me with stories of the early days of Hollywood in that soft, lisping voice of his.

Sadly, the film was not a very good one. I say 'sadly' because it was the last film Boris Karloff was to make; six months after he completed the picture, he died.

On the wall of my study as I write this I have a framed photograph of the great man which he gave me, at my request, at the end of the picture. It is inscribed, in a very shaky hand: *'To Mark. Who makes more bricks without straw than anyone I know of. Au revoir. Boris Karloff'*.

A few months later I did another film called Attack on the Iron Coast, a war film starring the American actor, Lloyd Bridges. Then, all through the summer I played the lead in a thirteen part TV series for ATV, called Crime Buster. It was about an investigative sports writer on a newspaper (me) who exposed corruption and shady dealings in all kinds of sport and it was on one of the episodes of this series that I was to meet my boyhood football hero, Billy Wright. In the days when loyalty was more important than financial gain, Billy Wright had spent his whole career with Wolverhampton Wanderers. He was capped for England 105 times, and captained England 90 times and one of the finest footballers this country ever produced. My biggest surprise on meeting him was seeing how small in height he was.

Back in the 1950's centre-halves (as they were called then) were all six feet tall and sometimes more. Billy Wright was about five feet nine inches! Considering his enormous sporting achievements he was a charming, modest man and we got on well working together.

At that time Billy was working at ATV as a sports commentator and had been engaged to play himself in an episode about an up-and-coming young footballer, played by John Alderton.

One day we were on location at Watford football ground. The scene was Billy and I sitting together watching the Watford team in practice with their new young signing. When the filming was over, some of the team came up and asked Billy if he would consider coming down onto the pitch for a short kick-about, so that they could say they had played football with Billy Wright. Billy was now in his mid 40's and a little overweight, but he sportingly agreed. Not to be outdone, I took off my coat and joined them. The kick-about only lasted about ten minutes I suppose, but when it was over I could honestly say I had played football with the great Billy Wright. As I say, it was a good year for me; but one that was to end in a sadness.

It was early November. I was having dinner alone one evening in a small Italian restaurant near to where I lived, when an attractive American girl came over to my table and asked for my autograph, explaining that she had seen me on TV the previous night. I invited her to sit down, we shared a bottle of wine, and ended up back at my flat in bed together. The following morning she flew back to America, and I finalised plans for a holiday, on my own, in the Canary Islands. My girlfriend, Patricia, had always had a set of keys to my apartment, and a few days before I was due back, let herself in to tidy up the place for my return. Unfortunately, among the mail lying on the doormat was a *postcard* from my American lady admirer thanking me for the 'wonderful night we spent together'. Patricia and I had always had a non-possessive kind of relationship, but there were limits, and I had overstepped them. We had been together for almost four years. Now it was over.

CHAPTER 17

GETTING MY KIT OFF
AND OTHER MISTAKES

It was in the summer of 1969 that I first went to a nudist colony. In the block of flats where I lived there was a wonderfully eccentric elderly man named Israel Sharman, whose tiny flat was stacked from floor to ceiling with books. He spoke six languages, and earned a living writing weighty tomes on arcane subjects and by translating. He was also a committed naturist, always extolling the virtues of nudism and the wonderful sense of freedom to be enjoyed as soon as those restricting clothes of ours were cast off. He had a girlfriend called Olga who was much younger than him and a little bit strange, but nice enough, and they both belonged to a nudist camp in Watford called, incongruously, Spielplatz.

Anyway, one sunny Sunday morning the phone rang. It was Izzy. He and Olga were going to drive out to Spielplatz that afternoon, and why didn't I come along with them? On an impulse I said yes. I thought it might be fun, all those bouncing bums, bobbing boobs, and waggling willies. Yes, why not? On the way out there though, I began to entertain second thoughts about the advisability of what I was doing. I mean, there I'd be, a red-blooded young-ish man surrounded by naked women; what if...?

As alcohol was not allowed in Spielplatz I made Izzy stop off at a pub, where I downed several large drinks in a short space of time in an effort to bolster my rapidly waning bravado, and perhaps help to quell any baser instincts that might rear their ugly heads. As it turned out I needn't have worried. Nudism proved to be the biggest turn-off since the power workers strike of 1958! The sad but inescapable fact is that 90% of adult human beings look absolutely ghastly without their clothes on, bringing home to me what a well-cut suit and good foundation garments can do to disguise any physical imperfections. But worse was to come. As the sky clouded over and the sun disappeared, a chill wind began to make itself felt. The first thing was the goose pimples that erupted all over my body which, on my pale skin, made me look rather like a freshly plucked, oversized chicken. However, the real damage was down in the meat and two veg department.

What, in the warmth of the sun, might modestly have been described as two walnuts and a medium-sized sausage had, in the brisk north-easterly, shrunk down to two prunes and a chipolata. Unable to take any more disillusionment and rapidly losing my dignity, I threw my clothes on and fled Spielplatz; never to return. I know it sounds pathetic to women, but our genitals are a very sensitive area; in more ways than one. None of us ever being satisfied with our allotted dimensions; always lamenting the lack of that extra inch which would have put us up there with the big nobs.

With some of us it can become a fixation, a friend of mine back then being a perfect example. He was a young actor who, to spare his blushes, I shall call John. He was tall, dark, and handsome with a good physique, a charming manner, and a smile that made women go week at the knees. There was, however, one dark cloud in his otherwise sun-lit life; he was convinced his penis was undersized. No matter how often we told him that it wasn't the *size* that is important, it is what you *do* with it, he remained dissatisfied with his lot; or in his case – *not* a lot.

One night, in his cups, he told me the following story; which I must say must have made him even more paranoid about his wee willy winkie. Arriving late at a party one night he was immediately pounced upon by one of the most attractive women he had ever met. She was almost six feet tall with flaming red hair, green eyes, and a figure of mind-blowing voluptuousness. She was Russian, and a painter, a flamboyant and bewitching enchantress who, in no time at all, had whisked John back to her studio and plied him with copious quantities of neat vodka. Eventually, she drained her glass, stood up and said: "Com, now ve mek luff." John, fearing he might not quite come up to the Russian redhead's wilder expectations, said: "Before we do, there's something I ought to tell you...I have a rather small penis." At this, the dominatrix was taken aback. "I don't believe it," she cried. "Show me. Show me," so John, reluctantly, took out his dick. In the silence that followed John heard himself say: "You see, this is my tragedy." "Darlink," she sighed, "that's not your tragedy. That's your comedy!"

The only other time I appeared naked in front of complete strangers, ended in an even more undignified exit than my trip to the nudist colony. It was the 'swinging sixties' and everyone was busy throwing off the shackles of middle-class mores and morality, none, I have to say, more enthusiastically than me. On the night in question a lady friend had asked me to accompany her to a party at a large house in the Primrose Hill area of London, which turned out to be a rather dreary affair. As the evening progressed so did my intake of alcohol, until I had reached the stage where rational thought had been replaced by wild imaginings.

As I looked around the assembled company through bloodshot eyes I decided that what this party needed was something of an outrageous or spectacular nature to liven things up. So I went upstairs to one of the bedrooms, took off all my clothes, and came back down again wearing nothing but an inane grin. By the time I reached the bottom of the stairs all conversation had ceased, and an appalled silence had fallen upon the slack-jawed guests.

This wasn't at all what I had expected. Gasps of outrage perhaps, laughter possibly, cheers maybe, even hoots of derision. Anything but a wall of silence. As I stood there wondering what I could do for an encore, a crimson-faced woman detached herself from the transfixed crowd, walked over to me and smacked my face so hard that I literally saw stars. Realising all too late that perhaps I had made a slight error of judgement, I turned around and, with as much aplomb as is possible in such a bizarre situation, waddled back up the stairs, hastily got dressed, and then made a run for it. My lady friend never spoke to me again.

By the end of 1969 I was still earning good money but, ignoring Mr Micawber's advice on the perils of annual expenditure exceeding annual income, had thrown myself into the nightlife of London with never a thought for the morrow. No surprise then when, in 1970, due in part to my profligacy but mostly because of my (then) accountant's criminal incompetence(he ended up serving two years in prison) bankruptcy proceedings were taken out against me by the Inland Revenue, to whom I owed £1,000 in back tax. It was an ignominious end to a decade in which I had had my share of both success and misfortune.

CHAPTER 18

THE FAMILY MAN

In the autumn of 1971 I was offered a part in a play called Conduct Unbecoming that was going out on tour for three months. I had always disliked touring and the money was lousy, so my first reaction was to turn it down. But, given the parlous state of my finances at that time, wiser counsels prevailed and, reluctantly, I accepted. Once again, fate had taken a hand in the direction my life was to follow, because it was on that tour that I met the woman who was to become my second wife and present me with the daughter I had always longed for.

Her name was Diana. She was 18 years younger than me, separated from her husband, and with a three year old son named Saul. About three weeks into the tour we fell in love, and spent the next nine weeks together. When we returned to London, Diana to Balham and I to Bloomsbury, we met up as often as we could. But my theory about 'on tour' romances cooling in the harsh light of reality, seemed about to happen to us, until...one evening in late February 1972 Diana rang me to say she was pregnant, and that call changed everything. On the 4th of November that year, at the Weir Hospital in Balham at around mid day, our daughter Polly Emma Joanie Winsome was born.

It was a Saturday, and I was rehearsing a TV play in Twickenham when the call came through that Diana had gone into hospital. By the time I got there I had just missed the birth, and when I first held her in my arms I thought her the most beautiful thing I had ever seen. Within a couple of months I had given up my flat in Bloomsbury, moved in with Diana, and at the rather advanced age of 44 found myself with a young wife and family to provide for. In spite of my initial apprehension and self-doubt I took to parenting like a duck to water and, although I say so myself, became pretty good at it. Bringing up Polly and Saul became such a happy and fulfilling experience, that it brought home to me the precious years I had lost by not being there for my son David.

About six weeks after Polly had been born I went to see our family doctor about a persistent cough I had developed. Dr Nurock was one of the old school GPs. He was charming, caring and committed. Qualities not found too often nowadays. After examining me, he asked how many cigarettes I smoked a day. I told him the truth, at least 40, sometimes more. He then asked me about my newly-born daughter. When I had finished rhapsodising about her, he said: "Let me tell you something. If you want to live to see your daughter grow up and have children of her own you have to stop smoking *now*. Not tomorrow or the next day. Do it for your daughter, and do it now." I can remember standing outside in the car park for some time thinking about what he had said. Then I took a half-full packet of King Size from my shirt pocket, crumpled it up and threw it into a litter bin. Since that day I have never smoked again.

On Friday 22nd of March 1973 Diana and I were married at Caxton Hall, with my ex-wife Joan as matron-of-honour. David, Saul and Polly were there plus my mum and dad, and my best man was our friend Nigel Plaskitt. It was a low key affair with just some drinks and sandwiches at a nearby hotel, because we were trying to get the money together to buy our own home. A few months later I began rehearsals for a six part TV serial of Dorothy L.Sayers' Clouds of Witness for the BBC, with Ian Carmichael playing Lord Peter Wimsey, and yours truly as his brother-in-law Detective Inspector Parker.

With more adaptations of her books in prospect, it was the financial fillip we had been waiting for, in that we could now afford the money for the deposit on a house.

Subsequently, we took out a mortgage and bought a three bed-roomed house in Mandrake Road, Tooting, just across the road from a school that both our kids were later to attend. The house cost £9,000, which was cheap even by house prices of the time, but for one very good reason. It was almost derelict. There was no bathroom and no indoor lavatory. The roof needed attention, the whole house needed re-wiring, there was rising damp, and an infestation of woodworm. Unable to afford to pay for anything but the most difficult of the jobs, Diana and I borrowed DIY books from the library, hired tools and machinery and did a great deal of the work ourselves. Working from the instructions and diagrams in one of the books, I re-wired the whole house, only getting in a qualified electrician at the end to check the wiring on all the sockets and to connect us to the mains.

We sanded all the floorboards, laid a tiled floor in the kitchen and painted the whole place from top to bottom. After six months of back-breaking work we had our own home, and the kids both had their own bedrooms and a small back garden to play in. It was while I was still working on the house that I heard I had landed a big TV commercial for TWA, the American airline. Actually, it was three commercials, all to be shot at Kennedy Airport in New York. I was actually painting a ceiling when the call came through from my agent telling me to go to the American Embassy in Grosvenor Square the next day to obtain a visa.

Three days later I was sitting in the first class cabin of a TWA jumbo jet, being plied with champagne and caviar in the company of two other actors; Christopher Reeves and Yul Bryner! Upon arrival in New York a limousine was waiting to whisk me to the Plaza Hotel where I was given a suite overlooking Central Park, and told to put everything 'on the tab'. It was a sudden and bewildering change of fortune, and another reminder of how an actor's life can be transformed, literally overnight.

When I went down to the famous Oak Room bar on the first night for a pre-prandial drink a woman was sitting at the bar on her own. She was in her mid to late thirties I guess, well dressed, and wearing very little make-up on what the Americans call a 'homely' face.

When I ordered my drink she said something to me about my English accent, and we got chatting.

During the conversation she shifted uneasily on her stool and I asked her if she was ok.

She said: "Yes. I'm a hundred dollars." Now, I have always thought of myself as fairly streetwise, and I thought what she had just said was a variation on the American expression: "I feel like a million dollars," only more modest. So I said: "Oh, that's good"' She said: "Well?" And I said: "Well what?" She said: "Is that ok with you?" So I said: "Is what ok with me?" She looked at me oddly for a moment, then (*sotto voce*) said: "I'm a working girl!" And finally the penny dropped –along with my jaw I suspect. So I mumbled something about having another appointment, finished my drink and left; feeling slightly less of an *homme du la monde* than when I came in. During my stay in New York the people I was working for took me out sightseeing at the weekend, and to dinner one night at the Cafe Carlyle to hear the famous pianist and singer, Bobby Short. When my two week visit came to an end I had my last taste of luxury on the plane coming home, then it was back to the real world again. Later that same year I appeared in two more TV adaptations of the Lord Peter Wimsey novels, Murder must Advertise and An Unpleasantness at the Bellona Club. Both were highly successful, and sold all over the world. Even now, over 35 years on, I still occasionally receive a royalty cheque because one of them has been has been shown somewhere.

In 1975 I did my first Situation Comedy. It was a thirteen-part series for LWT called The Top Secret life of Edgar Briggs, starring a young up-and-coming actor named David Jason. He was the Edgar Briggs of the title; an inept Secret service agent, and I was his long-suffering side-kick. It was produced by Humphrey Barclay and directed by Bryan Izzard, and was very funny. David Jason is a brilliantly inventive comic actor and rehearsals were enormous fun as we explored the comic possibilities of the script, and thought up new comedy business for the show. Unfortunately, when it came to transmitting the series the programme schedulers made a calamitous misjudgement.

They put the show out at the same time as an enormously popular, long-running serial on BBC called The Brothers which completely blew any chance of it achieving good viewing figures.

The critics loved it, and so did the viewers – the few that watched it, but it didn't get the audience LWT had anticipated so it was dropped. We were all bitterly disappointed, none more so than our producer, who had virtually promised us another series, so confident was he of its success.

Incidentally, I once asked Humphrey Barclay if he would stand in Nightingale Square in Balham and sing a few bars of music, so that I could say: "I heard a Barclay sing in Nightingale Square." A request he politely declined.

In 1976 I went out to Tunisia to appear in Jesus of Nazareth, Lew Grade's multi-million dollar epic. Like most big budget movies, when I got out there all was confusion. I was hanging around for three weeks, in a five star hotel in Monastir, before anyone even knew I had arrived. I had gone there to play one of the Roman soldiers who diced for the robe of Jesus at the foot of the cross, only to find that Franco Zefferelli, the director, had decided to cut the scene altogether. On my first day, not really knowing what to do with me, they strapped me into a roman soldier's uniform and told me to hang around at the location in case Il Duce (Zefferelli) might find something for me to do.

After a couple of days kicking my heels I got fed up with being treated like an extra, so I went back to base, took off my armour and went back to my hotel. It took them another three weeks to find me again, by which time I had visited several places of interest, including Carthage, and acquired a deep sun tan sitting around the pool. It was a strange set up. Half of British Actors Equity seemed to be there playing all the main parts (Jesus, the disciples, etc) with all the cameo roles being played by stars of international status.

James Mason was in the room next to me, I had a photograph

taken with Rod Steiger, I did a couple of scenes with Stacey Keach, and met Lawrence Olivier again.

Boredom was our biggest enemy. Being a Muslim country there wasn't much in the way of entertainment. In fact there was none at all, come to think about it, and the only place you could obtain alcohol was in your hotel.

So every night was spent playing cards or getting drunk (sometimes both) and on Sundays playing a football match against the hotel waiters, which we invariably lost. I was in Tunisia for almost three months altogether, and although the money came in handy I was more than happy to get back to my family, especially my little girl, who kept wrapping her arms around my leg every time I moved to stop me going away again.

Diana's parents lived near Darlington in County Durham. Her father was a farmer and in the summer holidays we would take the kids up to the farm and let them run wild; which they loved. Polly loved her 'ma-ma', Diana's mother, and they were very close. Sadly, early in 1978 she was diagnosed with advanced breast cancer, and soon became very ill. That same year we were told that my father had cancer of the throat, and he was admitted to hospital for treatment. Unfortunately it failed to halt the spread of the disease, and after a couple of months we were told there was nothing more the doctors could do, so he came home. When her mother's condition worsened, I looked after the children while Diana went up to Darlington to be with her. A week later she died. On the day of her funeral I left the kids with friends and went up to Darlington for the interment, and returned the same day.

Three months later on the 15th of September, twelve days after his 78th birthday, my father died. He left twenty pounds and a pair of gold cuff-links we had given him for his birthday. Not much to show for a lifetime of hard work, but then my dad had never been much interested in material things, the spiritual side of his life always being far more important.

In fact he once confided in me that, given the opportunity, he would gladly have renounced all worldly things, entered a monastery and lived a life of contemplation and prayer. On the day of his funeral we had a requiem mass said for him and laid him to rest in Finchley cemetery next to my brother Eddie; with his prayer book by his side and his rosary in his hands. Whenever I think of my father, as I often do, the last three verses of Gray's Elegy always come to mind. They are entitled 'The Epitaph', and seem to me to be a fitting one for my dear old dad.

Here rests his head upon the lap of Earth
A youth, to fortune and to fame unknown;
Fair science frown'd not on his humble birth,
And melancholy mark'd him for her own.
Large was his bounty, and his soul sincere;
Heaven did a recompense as largely send:
He gave to misery all he had, a tear,
He gain'd from heaven ('twas all he wished) a friend.

No farther seek his merits to disclose,
Or draw his frailties from their dread abode,
(There they alike in trembling hope repose)
The bosom of his Father and his God.

The following year I went into Coronation Street for the first time. They were looking for someone to play a lorry driver who has a brief romance with Elsie Tanner (Pat Phoenix) and I was offered the part. It was only a six week engagement but welcome nevertheless because, apart from the money, it enabled me to renew acquaintance with Tony Booth with whom I had lost touch over the years. He had survived a horrific accident in which he was badly burned, and the break up of his marriage, and was now re-united with Pat Phoenix, with whom he had been romantically linked some years before.

It's always a bit difficult going into a long-running TV series, so it helped that I already knew Johnny Briggs from way back and that I had worked with Bill Roache before he went into Coronation Street. In the autumn of 1960 Bill and I had appeared in a TV play at Granada called Marking Time, about a group of soldiers in the army of occupation in post-War Germany. One day in the canteen I asked Bill if he had any work coming up after the play was finished. He told me that he had been offered a three-episode try-out of a new northern based drama series called Florizel Street. "It's only about six weeks work," he said! I only mention this because the young actress who played Bill's girlfriend in those first episodes was Patricia Shakesby, who was to become my girlfriend in real life five years later.

1980 was the year I did a stage play with the Oscar-winning American actress, Gloria Grahame. David Thacker later became a director at The National Theatre, but at that time was running the Duke's Playhouse in Lancaster. Somehow he had persuaded Gloria Grahame to come there to do two plays: Who's afraid of Virginia Woolf by Edward Albee, and The Glass Menagerie by Tennessee Williams. The Albee play was the first to be produced and David Thacker had asked me to play George opposite Gloria Grahame's Martha. The pay was Equity minimum, £180 pounds a week, which meant I would have to find cheap digs for the duration. However, I would be working with one of the best young directors in the country, *and* a movie legend. How could I refuse? During rehearsals Gloria was taken ill, but insisted we continued rehearsing sitting around her bed – which we did for two or three days until she felt better. She tried to make light of the pain in her stomach that had laid her low, calling it 'a little female trouble', but in fact it was the cancer that was to end her life less than six months later. The two other characters in the play, Nick and Honey, were played brilliantly by Matthew Marsh and Leslie Nightingale, and the opening night was a huge success ending with a five minute standing ovation.

After a three week run, playing to packed houses, it was all over. It had been one of the most challenging roles I had ever attempted, but at the same time one of the most satisfying. Gloria Grahame never got to play Amanda Wingfield in The Glass Menagerie. Six months later she died of stomach cancer at the home of her boyfriend in Liverpool. Apparently she had refused orthodox medical treatment, putting her faith in 'alternative' medicine; and when told she had just a few days to live is reported to have said: "Don't be silly. Film Stars don't die in Liverpool." Sic transit Gloria. Sadly, by 1982 cracks were beginning to appear in our marriage. There was no one major reason for this as I recall, more an accumulation of minor ones, but we put aside our differences for the sake of the children, and carried on

In May 1983, in one last attempt to save our marriage, we took the kids on holiday to a house in St Margaret's Bay on the Kent coast, owned by our friend Miriam Margolyes. Sadly it didn't work out, and on our return to London we decided that the time had come for us to part. It was a heart-rending decision for me. Polly was ten years old and Saul 14, but we both agreed that it would be better in the long run for them to be spared the constant rows we had been having. So, after ten years our marriage was over, and I became deeply depressed. Not so much for the marriage itself, but for the effect it would have on the children. I felt I had let them down, and for a long time was racked with guilt and with that sense of failure that always seems to follow, so that when Bill Kenwright offered me a ten week tour – I jumped at it. It was a rotten play, and the money wasn't anything to write home about either, but I needed to get away for a while and try to sort my life out.

Our last port of call was The Greenwich Theatre in south east London, and it was while we were there that I received an invitation to an old friend's 40th birthday party, which I thought I might go to after the show. It was Saturday the 31st of July, and as I was driving back from Greenwich I began to have second thoughts. It was around 11.15pm and I had just done a matinee and an evening performance of a long and tedious play; the last thing I felt like doing was going to a party.

CHAPTER 19

WHEN MARK MET SUE

I still remember clearly, waiting at that set of traffic lights in Tooting trying to make up my mind whether to turn left and go to the party, or go straight on home; when the lights changed I turned left. It is a sobering thought that it is on such slender threads that the fabric of our lives can sometimes hang, because it was at that party I was to meet the woman with whom I have spent the last 27 years of my life. When I arrived I wished our host, Leo Dolan, a happy birthday, and – it being a warm summer night – went out into the garden. After chatting to a few friends for a while I became aware of a tall, slender, blonde haired woman standing under a cherry tree talking to someone. She was wearing a white dress, and was tanned, elegant, radiant and beautiful. I was smitten.

Seeing the theatrical agent Barry Brown was there with his wife Ros, I asked him if he knew who she was. "Her name is Sue Nicholls," he informed me in that mellifluous voice of his, adding, "and I'm her agent." "Ah," I said. "Will you introduce me to her?"
"*I* will," said Ros, and taking me by the arm, led me over and did just that.

And not a moment too soon, because Sue was just about to leave. She had come with two friends, in their car, and they were impatient to be off. Somehow before she went I managed to get her telephone number and a vague promise that we might meet up sometime. I have to say I found my behaviour that night puzzling to say the least, because at that particular time in my life the very *last* thing I was looking for was another relationship.

I rang Sue several times over the next few weeks to try to fix up a date, but she always seemed to be busy, and I began to think I was being given the old heave-ho. However, I decided to give it one last try – and this time she said yes! She had been invited to a friend's birthday barbeque and wondered if I would like to accompany her. The friend's name? Nigel Plaskitt; the best man at my marriage to Diana!

From the moment I picked Sue up at her Hampstead flat I realised she was someone special, and by the end of that evening I knew I had found a soul mate. We quickly discovered that we had the same sense of humour. On the drive over to the barbeque in Sue's car I made her laugh so much she had to pull over in a lay-by, for fear of crashing the car. From thereon in we spent the rest of the day laughing, something I hadn't done for a while; and love began to bloom.

After several months of seeing each other constantly, I had fallen deeply in love with her and she with me, and we began to discuss the idea of living together. This was a very big step for Sue. She was, and is, a fiercely independent woman; and had lived on her own since the age of 18.

It was to be *her* flat we would be living in, with all the difficult adjustments to her life this would entail. She was offering me love, support and security, but still I hesitated. I was still living (separately) in the marital home, and it would mean leaving the children.

I was terribly unsure of myself at that time, afraid of making a commitment I couldn't live up to. When I look back I can see how pathetic I must have been, but that's how I felt at the time. So that when an offer of a play at Harrogate came along, I thought it might be good for me to get away for a while, and give myself time to think. The play was Educating Rita, a two-hander by Willie Russell, with Sue Jenkins (who I was to work with later in Coronation Street) playing Rita.

At the beginning of November, just before rehearsals began, I went down to Ramsgate to see John Le Mesurier, for what turned out to be the last time. He had been desperately ill with cirrhosis of the liver, and was not expected to survive much longer. He was propped up in his hospital bed, his face pale and gaunt; and as I took his hand he said: "My dear fellow, you've grown a beard." "I'm playing a college professor." I said: "I thought it might make me look a bit more intellectual." "And has it?" John asked, with just the wisp of a mischievous smile.

Two weeks later, on November 15th, in the middle of rehearsals, I received a telephone call from Joanie telling me that John had died. Apparently his last words to her were; "It's all been rather lovely my darling, but I'm fed up of it now, and I want to go."
He was a lovely man, shy, charming, wistful and funny. I only wish that he and Sue could have met; they would have adored each other. Rehearsals were suspended for two days to allow me to go to John's funeral. All John's favourite songs were played, Bill Pertwee told some very funny stories about their time together in the TV series Dad's Army, and I read a loving tribute written by his good friend Derek Taylor.

The most poignant moment came at the end. John had once read a short poem at a friend's memorial service, and had been so taken by it that he had recorded it on an album he made with Derek Taylor called What's Going To Become of us All? It was the last voice we heard before the curtains closed around his coffin. John speaking his own epitaph.

> *When I am dead cry for me a little.*
> *Think of me sometimes,*
> *But not too much.*
> *Think of me now and again as I was in life,*
> *At some moment it is pleasant to recall;*
> *But not for long.*
> *Leave me in peace, and I shall leave you in peace.*
> *And while you live let your*
> *Thoughts be with the living.*

It wasn't until the last two days of the play that Sue drove up to Harrogate to see me. Because of my stupidity and fear of commitment Sue was having serious doubts about the long-term prospects of our relationship, but had decided to give it one last try. It was an act of faith on her part which I will always love her for; because it finally brought me to my senses and made me realise how much I needed her in my life. Her visit wasn't all plain sailing though. On the last night we had supper in a small Italian bistro where, for some reason now long forgotten, we had a blazing row. However, by the time we set off to drive to London the next morning we had agreed to live together and see how it worked out. It was a decision for which I have never ceased to thank Providence.

I spent one last Christmas with my children, and in January 1984, six months after our first meeting, I moved all my personal belongings – plus some odd pieces of furniture – into Sue's flat. Sue had already met Diana, so I took her down to Ramsgate to meet my other ex, Joanie. It was to be a meeting of like-minds, and they immediately became firm friends. While we were there Sue met Joan's parents, Fred and Nellie Long. Fred had been ill for some time with cancer of the jaw, an affliction which had disfigured his face and impaired his speech, but not his wonderful sense of humour. On our return to London I took Sue to meet my family, all of whom adored her, especially my mother.

I remember mum buttonholing me as I came out of the loo after that first meeting and saying to me: "Sue is the best thing that has ever happened to you. She is a wonderful girl, and if you do the dirty on her you'll have me to reckon with!"

The following Easter Sue took me to meet her parents. Lord and Lady Harmar Nicholls lived in a large rambling, early Victorian mansion in rural Staffordshire, called Abbeylands, where I was welcomed with such warmth and hospitality that by the end of my stay I already felt like one of the family. Unfortunately, the warmth of my welcome was not matched by the temperature inside the house itself. Twelve large rooms, high ceilings, draughty windows, long corridors – and no central heating! None of your namby-pamby, overheated rooms that we effete southerners expect. This was the Black Country, and thick sweaters were the order of the day – and night!

I remember one particularly cold Christmas we were staying at Abbeylands. Sue and I had been out for a brisk walk around the village, and as we turned for home I started to take off my overcoat. "What are you doing?" said Sue, with puzzled look and furrowed brow. "I'm taking off my overcoat," I said. "Otherwise I won't feel the benefit of it when I get in the house!" A slight exaggeration, but not by very much.

Having got all the formalities out of the way we settled down to our life together, neither of us looking too far into the future, taking each day as it came.

In March 1985 my ex father-in-law finally lost his long, unequal battle with cancer. Although we had long since ceased to be related by marriage I still considered myself to be part of the family, and had always been treated as such. I wrote my own tribute to Fred which I read in the same chapel where, fourteen months earlier, I had done the same for John Le Mesurier. The loss of her husband and her father in such a short space of time had a profound effect on Joan. The following summer, unable to cope with the many painful memories and sad reminders, Joan left Ramsgate where, in her own words: "Everything around me had a history; and every street led me back into the past", and went to live in Spain.

She bought a large *casa antiqua* in a small seaside town on the Costa Dorada called Sitges, surrounded herself with several stray cats, and in an act of catharsis, wrote her frank, funny, sad and uplifting autobiography, Lady Don't Fall Backwards.

In the summer of 1985 Joan invited Sue and I over to stay with her; and we immediately fell in love with Sitges. Back then it was a small, undiscovered seaside town, with very few English people; which meant that we could wander around unnoticed. So taken were we with the place that we ended up buying a penthouse apartment with a large wrap-around balcony. Sadly, as both our workloads in Coronation Street increased we spent less and less time there and, eventually, sold the apartment. We still go back to Sitges at least once a year; usually in September when the weather is a little cooler and the crowds have thinned out a bit.

CHAPTER 20

CORONATION STREET

Towards the end of 1985 Sue was asked to join the cast of Coronation Street on a regular basis. Since 1979 she had been intermittently playing the part of the mother of one of the characters in the show, now they wanted her character to become a permanent one. It would mean us being separated for the first time, but we both agreed that it was too good an offer to turn down.

As it turned out, it was to prove a fortuitous decision because six months later, in one of those happy coincidences that sometimes light up our lives, I was asked to join the cast of Coronation Street as well to play a character called Alan Bradley. In the acting profession it is seldom, if ever, that couples get the chance to work with each other, with us it was to last almost four years.

The first few days of rehearsal on any new job is a period of adjustment, and although I had already worked with some of the cast before it took me a little while to settle in, and to get to know the actress who was to play opposite me, more or less, for the next three and a half years. Barbara Knox, who plays Rita, is a charming, funny lady, a wonderful raconteur and a superb actress and we got on famously. The producer of Coronation Street at that time was the late, and much lamented, Bill Podmore, or 'Podders' as he was affectionately known. A lovely man, approachable, considerate, and hugely popular with the cast. I think it's fair to say though that Bill 'liked a drink', and it was common knowledge among the cast that if you needed to talk to him about anything important it was advisable to do so before he went to lunch. Bill had always been fairly flexible about the interpretation of the words 'lunch' and 'hour'. In Bill's view lunch was a movable feast. It could start as early as 11.45 am and, depending on the conviviality of the company, sometimes finish as late as 4pm; and thereby hangs a cautionary tale. A few years back Barbara had made the mistake of going to see Bill after he had partaken of a long, over-indulgent lunch.

She was seeking his permission to take the following Wednesday off to go to Epsom for Derby Day. She explained to Bill that they had been offered a box in the Royal Enclosure and, as she had very little to do that week, would it be alright if she missed a day's rehearsal and enjoyed a day at the races? Nose and cheeks aglow, Bill was magnanimous. "Of course you can, Barbara,'" he beamed. "Leave it to me."

FADE:

Derby Day dawns; and a Rolls Royce whisks Barbara and her husband off to Epsom. Meanwhile, back at Granada Studios everyone is waiting for Barbara to arrive so that they can start rehearsals. Anxious phone calls to Barbara's house only get the answering machine. Bill is as puzzled as the others, and rehearsals proceed without Rita Fairclough. Being a sporting man, Bill was back in his office in time to watch the big race on TV. As the picture slowly materialised onto his screen there, before his disbelieving eyes, was Barbara in a large, picture hat and all her finery, quaffing champagne and laughing merrily; while the rest of the cast had their collective noses to the grindstone.

FADE:
MIX TO:

The next morning. Barbara swans into rehearsals, only to be met by an icy atmosphere and a curt summons to see Bill in his office – *immediately*!

"But Bill," Barbara wailed, when she managed to get a word in, "*You* gave me permission." "Never," roared Bill. "I would never agree to such a thing. Never."

It all blew over eventually, as these things do, but how had this misunderstanding occurred? The answer – as we who have supped with Bacchus and his pards know only too well – is a condition known as post-alcoholic amnesia, commonly known as 'boozers blank'. To those of you who have experienced this distressing condition, I need say no more. For those among you who haven't...it goes something like this:

You are at a party, say. Everything is fairly clear up to a certain point, then WHAM! A black hole opens up in your mind; and from then on it is oblivion. Nothingness. From the moment you prise open your bloodshot eyes the following morning; unanswered questions begin to spin around your aching head.

What happened? What time did I leave? How did I get home? And, most worrying of all, *who* is that lying beside me? In the sixties, whenever Tom Bell and I had been to a party together, he would ring me up the following morning to ask if he had insulted anyone. He usually had, so, armed with a list of names, he would take himself off to a local florist, buy several posies, call a cab and deliver a bouquet to those whose character he had impugned the previous night. 'Bunching them' he called it.

Always loved flowers, did Tom. He once told me that one of the most contented periods of his life was the three months he spent one summer working on the flower beds of a London Park.

Not surprisingly then, that it was Tom's passion for flowers that was to get him into trouble with the police. He was walking home late one night from his local pub, having had a drink or two.

As he wended his way home through the bosky glades of Hampstead, he was suddenly gripped by an overwhelming desire to take his (then) wife a bunch of flowers. So, emboldened by drink, he stepped into someone's front garden and proceeded to pick a posy of mixed blooms for his lady wife. Before you could say 'chrysanthemum', he found himself in the arms of three burly policemen and the jaws of an Alsatian dog.

Being a reasonable sort of chap, Tom took exception to what he considered an over-reaction on the part of the Old Bill, and put up a spirited resistance. As this unlikely quartet (to say nothing of the dog) surged back and forth across what had once been someone's neat front garden, Tom demanded to know why they weren't doing something useful, like feeling the collars of the many villains that roam London by night relieving people of their valuables.

This sort of remonstrance never cuts much ice with the boys in blue, and Tom very soon found himself face down in the back of a police wagon on his way to Rosslyn Hill nick.

He spent the night in a police cell, appeared before a magistrate next morning, and was fined £25 and bound over for six months.

To mark the event, I wrote a parody of a popular folk song of the day called Where have all the Flowers Gone? and sang it to Tom over the phone. It went like this:

> *Where have all the flowers gone?*
> *Judge kept asking.*
> *Where have all the flowers gone,*
> *Where did they go?*
> *Where have all the flowers gone?*
> *Tom Bell picked them every one.*
> *When will he ever learn?*
> *When will he ever learn?*

Yes, I know it's not very good, but it made me and many others laugh at the time. Tom thought it pathetic.

I have to say that Tom was not the easiest man to get on with. He could be extremely rude and dismissive to people he didn't like or respect, and was notoriously difficult to work with. He had precious few friends, but those he did have were, well, precious. And he clasped us to him with 'hoops of steel'. He was an intensely private person and at times could be taciturn and remote. But I think I understood him better than most and, more importantly, could make him laugh.

It was me who talked into having a dinner suit made for the

premiere of The L-Shaped Room, instead of hiring one from Moss Bros in Covent Garden. He agreed, with one condition: that I went with him and had one made myself. Consequently we both went along to Duggie Hayward, at that time THE showbiz tailor, where I chose a midnight blue barathea while Tom opted for the more conventional black. When we went back for the final fitting I asked Tom what he thought of my snazzy new dinner suit. "You look like a bloody band leader," he said. It was so typical of Tom that just as his star was in the ascendant, he almost wrecked his career with an alcohol-fuelled outburst at a celebrity-studded function where the Duke of Edinburgh was guest speaker.

The occasion was the 1963 BAFTA awards dinner at the London Hilton hotel. The L-Shaped Room had received a nomination and Tom had been coerced into attending. The table at which Tom and his then wife were sitting also boasted three famous married couples: Peter Hall and Leslie Caron, Richard Attenborough and Sheila Sim and Bryan Forbes and Nanette Newman. Tom always hated 'posh do's' like this and had drunk copiously throughout the dinner and the presentations. So by the time the Duke of Edinburgh rose to make his speech, Tom was well and truly rat-arsed. The Duke had only been speaking for five minutes when Tom suddenly called out: "Tell us a funny story."

At this there was a sharp intake of breath from the assembled glitterati, and all heads turned to see who had committed this act of *lese majeste*. The Duke of Edinburgh appeared unfazed by the interruption. "If you wanted funny stories," he said, "perhaps you should have engaged a comedian." Not to be outdone, Tom replied loudly: "I thought we had!" By now the room was bristling with indignation as two grim-faced security men arrived at the table where the others were sitting in shell-shocked disbelief, lifted Tom bodily out of his chair and, to a round of applause, escorted him out of the room.

Later on, when Leslie Caron apologised to the Duke of Edinburgh for Tom's behaviour, HRH, being the man he is, made light of the incident, remarking that the young man was 'probably a little merry'. Others were not so forgiving. After finishing The L-Shaped Room, Tom had signed a three-year exclusive contract with Beaver Films for more movies. Under the terms of that contract they had to pay him, but they never employed him again.

Now, here's a funny thing. Of the three men sitting at the table that night, Richard Attenborough was knighted and then made a Lord and Peter Hall has received a knighthood; both richly deserved; but what of Bryan Forbes? Throughout the 1960s and beyond Bryan was one of the most successful writer/directors the British film industry ever produced. His body of work speaks for itself: The L-Shaped Room, Séance on a Wet Afternoon, The League of Gentlemen, Whistle Down The Wind, The Angry Silence, King Rat, to name but a few. Many of those films have become cult classics. Not only did he direct them, he also wrote the screenplays as well, for which he was given a CBE. Not much reward really when you consider his enormous contribution to the cinematic arts. It is not too late; a knighthood would be a fitting tribute to a nice man and a truly great film director.

Within three months of my arrival in Manchester Sue and I had moved out of our rented accommodation, and bought a penthouse flat in a modern complex five minutes walk away from Granada Studios. Now that we were both working on the same show, it meant that we were together twenty four hours a day, every day.

It has been said that two people living in such close proximity to each other like that, over a prolonged period of time, is a recipe for marital disaster. All I can say is our relationship not only survived, it flourished, and continued so to do for the next three years. They were good years for us. Not only were we appearing in the most popular show on British TV, and earning a very good living doing it, but also we were invited to countless dinners and functions, interviewed, photographed, wined dined and feted.

The other side of the coin, of course, is the complete lack of privacy. Once you start to appear regularly on a show like Coronation

Street you become, in a sense, public property, and wherever you go you are subjected to instant recognition and requests for photographs and/or autographs. After a while I began to realise that autograph hunters, broadly speaking, fall into three categories: the professional, the apologetic and the ungracious. The 'professional' is invariably, but not always, male; and is to be found outside every gala dinner, grand opening, charity ball or first night. He usually comes equipped with a camera and a cluster of differently coloured pens. Apart from his autograph book he also carries a small archive of old photographs, theatre programmes and press cuttings for you to sign. What is more, he can tell you the very first film you ever appeared in, who directed it and who did the location catering! They're a wee bit worrying, those professionals. The 'apologetic' is usually female, who tells you all about her family before asking you for an autograph, expressing the hope that she is not putting you to too much trouble. The 'ungracious' is exclusively male. Determined not to be impressed, he usually approaches you in a pub or a restaurant, slaps down a piece of a menu or a torn-off bit of a cigarette packet in front of you and says: "Stick your name on there for us, pal. It's not for me, I never watch the programme meself; it's for the missus. Soppy as a two-bob watch, her. Make it out to Doreen, can you? Oh, and you'd better put 'Alan Bradley' after your name else she won't know who you are."

There are always the oddballs of course, those who defy categorisation, and it was one of these that Julie Goodyear, who played Bet Lynch in Coronation Street, met one day. Julie was having lunch in a restaurant with a friend when she became aware that every time she caught the eye of the woman sitting opposite she would smile conspiratorially and nod her head in a knowing manner. Quite often this kind of facial semaphore is the precursor to a request for an autograph, but to Julie's relief it didn't happen.

With the meal over they paid the bill and Julie went to the Ladies' room. She had no sooner settled down when there was a knock on the cubicle door and a woman's voice said: "Bet, while you're not doing anything, would you sign this for me?" A hand appeared under the door holding a pencil and a piece of paper. Being the trouper she is Julie signed her name and passed the paper and pencil back under the door.

The other side of the coin is, of course, the invitations you get to Premieres, First Nights and other grand occasions. It was at one such black tie function that the delightful Joanna Lumley, who appeared in Coronation Street herself at one time, came over and asked if she could have a photograph taken with Sue and me! When I gave one of those photos to my mother she was so taken with it that she had it framed and it took pride of place on her sideboard.

CHAPTER 21

TOURING THE FAR EAST

After I had been working on Coronation Street for almost a year, the actor/director John Fraser called my agent to ask two questions: 1)Would I be interested in doing a tour of the Far East playing Claudius in Hamlet, and 2) what were the chances of Granada releasing me to do it?. I had first met John Fraser a couple of years back when I worked on a series he was appearing in called The Practice and he had told me about the company he had set up with Delina Kidd and Gary Raymond called The London Shakespeare Group who, under the auspices of The British Council, took Shakespeare's plays all over the world. "You must come and do a play with us some time," he had said, and now, out of the blue, he had come up with this marvellous offer. The tour was to begin in Malaysia, then on to Japan, Hong Kong, Indonesia, Borneo and Thailand before finishing up in South Korea. It was chance to play a wonderful part in, arguably, Shakespeare's greatest play, and a once in a lifetime opportunity to visit all those exotic, far-flung places. It was almost too good to be true, but would Granada allow me to do it? Our producer at that time was John Temple, and I went along to see him more in hope than expectation. To my surprise he said he would think about it. Then, a week later, told me I could go. Two months later I was rehearsing Hamlet at the British Council building in Portland Place.

We left England in mid October, flew directly to Penang in Malaysia, and from there on to Japan. While we were in Japan we were accompanied everywhere by a nice man named Kenichi Watenabe, who acted as our guide and interpreter. It is one of those quirks of phonetics that the Japanese, when speaking English, have trouble with the letter 'L', always pronouncing it as an 'R'; which must make it difficult for them when the have an election! One night, after we had finished the play, Kenichi was waiting for us.

As we came back to our dressing rooms, over the Tannoy we could hear that the audience was still applauding. 'Risten,' said Kenichi proudly, 'they are still crapping'. In all we played six theatres and sixteen universities in seven different countries, all within the space of nine weeks. So that when I returned to England just before Christmas I was exhausted.

I had enjoyed it all immensely, but it was a relief to rest up for a few weeks before starting work on Coronation Street again.
When I returned to Granada change was in the air. Firstly John Temple had moved on to pastures new and Bill Podmore was back in charge again. Now that he was in the driving seat one more, Bill was planning a few changes, one of which was to radically alter the character I was playing. Up until now Alan Bradley had been a straightforward, ordinary sort of bloke with perhaps the slightest hint of mystery regarding his past. Now all that was about to change.

From now on, Bill informed me, Alan Bradley would be transformed into the most evil character ever to appear on Coronation Street. As I sat in Bill's office listening to all this I was beset by two conflicting emotions. On the one hand 'baddies' in Soaps are quite often the best parts, but on the other hand they also have a nasty habit of coming to a sticky end! However, the decision had already been taken, so I had no option but to go along with it.

And so the metamorphosis of Alan Bradley from man to monster began, slowly at first but accelerating as the viewing figures started to increase and more and more people got hooked on the storyline. As my character became more evil so the hate mail started to arrive, slowly at first, but building up rapidly with each outrage I perpetrated on the hapless Rita Fairclough. Barbara Knox was inundated with letters warning her about me, and begging her not to believe a word I said. It is quite amazing how seriously some people take Soaps, especially Coronation Street. All the performing arts demand a certain degree of suspension of disbelief from an audience, but television Soaps seem to trigger a complete acceptance from a section of viewers, usually, but not always, among the elderly or the housebound.

In August 1988 the Sun newspaper voted me 'Britain's Biggest Rat'. In a close-run contest I had apparently beaten off strong challenges from such villainous heavyweights as J.R Ewing of Dallas and Dirty Den in East Enders to emerge triumphant– if that is the word I want. I can't say it mattered all that much to me, but my mum wasn't too pleased. 'Britain's Biggest Rat' wasn't the kind of epithet she had in mind for me back in 1942 when I had reluctantly donned the blue serge uniform of a Post Office telegram boy. 'Britain's Proudest Postman' perhaps, or even 'Britain's Smartest Sorter', but Britain's Biggest Rat'? She wasn't very happy with that. As the story line progressed, and I became more and more obnoxious, the hate mail started to increase.

An elderly lady hit me on the head with her umbrella in Kendal's store in Manchester, incensed at my despicable treatment of Rita. Lorry drivers, who were pulled up at traffic lights, would shake their fists at me and threaten retribution if I didn't give Rita the money back that I had stolen from her, etc, etc. Matters finally came to a head the night I attempted to murder Rita in her own home, an episode that attracted an audience of almost 27 million! One of the highest viewing figures ever recorded for Coronation Street.

Because it was a very violent scene, Barbara and I carefully 'choreographed' the whole thing together – in slow motion – until we were absolutely sure of every move we were going to make in order to avoid any accidents. In a scene like that, with so much physical and emotional energy being expended, it is essential to get it in one take and thankfully we did. We were both so emotionally drained afterwards that I don't think either of us could have done it again. Apparently, when it was shown, the scene was so realistic that a self-help group called MOVE (Men overcoming violence (against women) asked Granada for permission to show a video of the scene to the men who attended their therapy sessions, to illustrate the disastrous consequences a sudden explosion of male rage can result in. After that I went on the run for a few weeks (in the story I mean) and was finally captured when the police followed my daughter (Sally Ann Matthews) when she came to meet me. I appeared in court, was remanded in custody at Risley Detention Centre, and Rita's nightmare was over...for the time being.

There, for the moment, my storyline came to a halt while the powers-that-be decided what would become of Alan Bradley. My own feeling was that I should receive a longish prison sentence, which would leave the way open for me to return when I had served my time, looking for revenge.

It was not to be. Unknown to me, at one of their quarterly meetings some of the writers proposed that I should be 'killed off'.

A vote was taken and the proposal was carried and endorsed, after some misgivings, by our producer Bill Podmore. I must say, Bill's attitude surprised me somewhat. He, more than anyone, should have known that killing off a character who had boosted the viewing figures to unprecedented heights made no sense. Apart from anything else, you could never know when you might need him again. Too late now though; the die had been cast. All that remained was for the writers to figure out how to dispose of Alan Bradley.

I knew nothing of all this at the time of course. While these discussions were going on I was enjoying a well-earned rest. I had gone over to Spain to stay with my ex wife Joan and, together with our son David, had begun to write a screenplay based on Joan's tragic love affair with the comedian Tony Hancock.

Six months later my agent received a call from the Coronation Street office asking me to go back into the series. The storyline was a cracker. By pleading guilty to the lesser charge of occasioning bodily harm Alan Bradley would walk free, the court having taken into account the time he had already spent on remand. Free to wreak revenge on the person responsible for putting him in prison, a terrified

Rita Fairclough. This time there was to be no physical violence; he was too cunning for that. It was to be all psychological: watching her constantly, following her wherever she went, making veiled threats etc, until she suffered a complete nervous breakdown.

All great stuff, and I couldn't wait to get back and get started. What I *didn't* know of course, and what they omitted to tell me, was that it was to end with my 'death'. Had I known, I'm not sure I would have returned. But I didn't know, so I did; go back I mean. Gradually though, as the story progressed, I began to suspect that that was their intention. Our producer at that time was Mervyn Watson, Bill Podmore having been shunted back to Executive Producer again, so I went along to see him. When I asked him straight out if I was to be killed off he was quite frank with me.

He told me when it would happen, but not how or where, in order to prevent the press from getting hold of it. So there it was. I can't honestly say I was all that upset about it, just angry at their discourtesy in not telling me beforehand. Over the next few months working with Barbara Knox again was a joy. She is such a fine actress, acting – and more importantly *re*acting – so brilliantly that some of our scenes together became quite frightening in their intensity. I remember after one particularly harrowing scene where I had reduced her to a sobbing, hysterical wreck, I went over to her afterwards and hugged her for two or three minutes until she had regained her composure. No surprise therefore, to me anyway, that in the November of 1989 she received the TV Times award for best actress.

All too soon the end was in sight; and in September of that year we travelled over to Blackpool to shoot my final scenes. Blackpool Corporation had been caught on the horns of a dilemma as far as my storyline was concerned. On the one hand the publicity generated would be very welcome, but it was the manner of my passing that had them worried. Blackpool trams have an enviable safety record, and Alan Bradley getting knocked over and killed by one might dent their image a bit. However, in the end they decided that the publicity was more important and, on the day, provided all the cooperation and support we needed.

On the final day hundreds of people had gathered on the seafront to watch the action, making it extremely difficult to shoot the scenes, what with all the noise and with crowds of people milling around. Eventually, after several hold-ups, we came to the final scene. I chased Rita across the road as she tried to escape from me, and ended up lying face down, having been run over by a number 10 tram.

On the night that episode was screened 26.93 million viewers tuned in to watch it, another record audience for Coronation Street. Apparently, the next day someone put up a plaque on the railings near to where I had been 'killed'. It read: "On this spot Alan Bradley, the sham, was hit and killed by a Blackpool tram." A few days later somebody pinched it!

Ever since it began back in 1960 there have always been real-life 'characters' in Coronation Street and during my time there were two. One was Bill Waddington who played Percy Sugden, and the other was Jill Summers, who played Phyllis Pearce.

Jill was a wonderful, blue-rinsed, elderly northern lady with a deep, gravelly voice, and a wicked sense of humour, who would regale us with stories of her years as a comedienne touring the country in Variety shows, and playing the working men's clubs. One of my favourite stories was when a man exposed himself to her one day. She was in her mid sixties at the time, but she stopped, smiled at the man and said: "Oh, you *are* a sport. I haven't seen one of them for years!"

Before coming into Coronation Street Bill Waddington had been a well known comedian, and in 1955 had appeared on the Royal Command Performance at the London Palladium. His was a wonderful character and he was great in the part, but there was one big problem - he could *never* remember his lines, which, of course, meant constant stoppages. To help him get through a scene Bill would place several *aides memoire* in strategic places on the set. For instance, if he had a scene in the Rover's Return, one of his favourite tricks was to write his lines on a couple of beer mats and leave them on the bar. The trouble was, that before he made his entrance other actors would either have moved them, (sometimes deliberately) or placed their drinks on them, thus rendering them illegible.

In one episode he had a scene in a doctor's surgery, and all through rehearsals could never remember certain medical ailments he had to mention, so he came up with what he thought was a brilliant idea. Before he went on he wrote down all the elusive words, in ink, on a piece of paper and Sellotaped it into his cap.

On cue Bill entered, took off his cap and placed it on his lap. The scene had hardly begun when the director called "Cut". "What," he asked over talk-back from the control gallery, "is *that* on Bill's head?" Closer inspection revealed that imprinted across Bill's bald pate were all the words he had so carefully written down!

CHAPTER 22

LIFE AFTER CORONATION STREET

The big question for me at this juncture in my life was, what do I do now? Having been identified for the past four years with such a high profile character in the most popular programme in Britain meant that television work would be hard to come by for a while, and I didn't really want to do any of the plays I was offered to take out on tour. I did do a pantomime at Christmas, playing the villain of course, and the following year appeared at the Malvern Festival playing Alfred Doolittle in Shaw's Pygmalion, which I enjoyed enormously; but more and more felt I needed a change of direction.

Consequently I bought a computer, got my friend Nigel Plaskitt to teach me how to work it and encouraged, as ever, by my darling Sue, tried my hand at writing. By 1993 Sue and I had been together for ten years. We had often discussed getting married, but for one reason or another had never got around to it. Partly, I think, because we both felt our relationship was working rather well as it was. But I was now 65, and becoming increasingly loath to introduce Sue to people as my 'partner'; or even worse my 'girl friend'.

So, knowing that Sue had some time off during the first two weeks of July, I took our birth certificates and all the other necessary documents down to The Registry department at Camden Town Hall in Euston Road, signed all the forms, put up the banns, and set a date for us to be married. As I was walking back up Euston Road it occurred to me that I wasn't very far away from the two schools in Somers Town that I had attended in my childhood.

Suddenly, seized by nostalgia and pricked by curiosity, I turned right into Charlton Street, then left into Phoenix Road and found myself, for the first time in almost 60 years, outside my old infant school. It seemed hardly to have changed in all that time, just smaller than I remembered. But then, all the places from ones childhood seem to have shrunk a little when revisited in later life. It was playtime, and the playground was swarming with shrieking, laughing little children, scampering and cavorting in the warm sunshine. Not much change there either, except for the kids themselves. These little ones were far less grimy than we were, and better fed and much better dressed than their scruffy, undernourished, 1930's predecessors.

I then walked the hundred or so yards up to St Aloysius Junior School, retracing the steps I and my classmates had taken with such excitement and high hopes in the Spring of 1935. The school not only looked smaller, but less forbidding than I remembered. I also remembered how, quite often, I had stood outside those very gates fighting back tears before going in to face the unforgiving, unforgivable, Mister Duffy.

I walked up Eversholt Street to Camden Town where I had misspent most of my adolescent years mindlessly hanging around its street corners. Up past the old Camden Hippodrome, now a Rock venue, passing the site where Alfred Kemp's second hand clothes emporium had once stood where, in 1953, I had bought my wedding suit for £3.15 shillings. I walked on past the bottom end of Delancey Street where the 'Regal' billiard hall of my youth was situated. At that time it was run by a character called Charlie (I never knew his other name) Charlie was probably in his fifties, had three or four blackened stumps in his mouth that served as his teeth, always wore a dirty, brown warehouseman's coat, and served a cup of tea the colour of Dark Oak varnish.

Just by looking at Charlie you could hazard a guess that hygiene had never been high on his list of priorities, either personally or proprietorially. Consequently, the Regal's lavatory was a fetid place, with a smell of such eye-watering, throat-constricting pungency that it was advisable to take a deep breath before going in, and not inhaling again until you had staggered out. I carried on up Camden High Street to where the Black & White Milk Bar had once been, and caught a number 31 bus to Swiss Cottage.

I hadn't been on a bus for some time, but it seems I was meant to catch that particular bus because at the very next stop my dear mother was standing. There she was, 90 years old, partially sighted and almost deaf, and carrying two carrier bags of groceries. Indomitable as ever, she told me she had 'got fed up of sitting indoors' and as it was a fine day had decided to go out shopping *on her own*! Not wanting the whole bus to be privy to my news while mum fiddled with her hearing aid, I waited until we got off the bus before telling her of our impending marriage. Bless her heart she was overcome with happiness and excitement, especially since she was the very first to be told.

That night I poured myself a glass of champagne before sitting down to ring Sue in Manchester. After telling her what I had done I said: "It's all set for July 6th at 3.45pm. Will you marry me?" There was silence for a moment, then Sue said: "How can I refuse, after such a romantic proposal?" She made only one stipulation. It was to be a *quiet* wedding. No announcement, no press, no fuss, and not even any family, just us and two witnesses.

And so on the appointed day five of us foregathered in the Registrars office at Camden Town Hall for my third and Sue's first, marriage. Those present were (once again) my first wife Joanie, her then partner Del Brown, and our old and dear friend Nigel Plaskitt. We made our vows, signed the register, and emerged into the afternoon sunshine as man and wife. A limousine was waiting to take us to the Waldorf Hotel in Aldwych where we had a wedding tea; two bottles of champagne, sandwiches and a small wedding cake. The following morning we flew to Guernsey for a three day honeymoon, then Sue went back to Manchester and Coronation Street, while I remained in London.

And that is how our lives have remained to the present day. Sue based in Manchester and me in London. We see each other as often as is possible in the circumstances, phone one another at least three or four times a day when we are apart, and always last thing at night. We make the most of our time together; going on holidays, to the theatre, to concerts etc. One day it will be the 'cottage in the country' for us perhaps, but not just yet. We both still have a lot of things to do.

In September 2000, after a short illness, Sue's father died at the age of 88. It was only a short time before Sue was due to fly to Paris to do some location filming for Coronation Street and Granada were caught on the horns of a dilemma. On the one hand, if the shoot was cancelled the knock on effect would play havoc with the schedules. Hotel rooms had been booked, locations secured, French extras engaged. New storylines would have to be written post haste, actors given time off would have to be recalled, etc, etc. On the other hand, they could hardly ask Sue to be out of the country when her father's funeral took place. As it turned out, Sue and her sister Judith took the decision to postpone the funeral until after Sue's return from Paris. It was a decision which must have come as a huge relief to Granada, even though I believe they were quite prepared to re-schedule the whole thing as a mark of respect.

Sue went to Paris as planned and, being the woman she is, played her scenes with John Savident (Fred Elliot) beautifully, with no hint of the sadness she must have been feeling.

At Lord Harmar's funeral service I read out a tribute to him which I had written, at Sue's request, which was well received. Six months later, I was invited to do the same thing at the Chapel of Saint Mary Undercroft in the Palace of Westminster at a Service of Thanksgiving for the Life and Work of The Baron Harmar-Nicholls. It was a great honour of course, but a bit nerve-wracking, in that everyone in the congregation was a Peer, a Peeress, a Right Honourable, an Honourable, a Venerable or a Reverend, and I was an out-of-work actor.

At around 12.35pm I was introduced by The Reverend Robert Wright, Rector of St Margaret's Church, climbed the spiral steps to the pulpit, looked out over the rows of upturned faces, and began by saying: "I suppose you're wondering why I called this meeting?" No, I didn't. That was a joke.

What I actually said was: "Lord Harmar-Nicholls was my father-in-law and I am very proud to have known him and to have been part of his family." Afterwards, several people came up to say 'well done' so I think I must have passed muster with the great and the good.

At this point it behoves me to tell you a little about my late father-in-law, because he was a man of great ability and quite exceptional achievement. Before he joined the army in 1940 - at the age of 28 - he had already been a successful businessman, a JP, and Chairman of the Darlaston Urban District Council. He joined The Royal Engineers regiment and, as a Lieutenant, spent the duration of the war in India and Burma.

On his demobilisation he studied Law, was called to the bar, but never practised as a barrister, because by then he had decided to be a politician. Subsequently, in 1950 he entered the House of Commons as the Conservative MP for Peterborough; with a majority of just three!

Ten years later, after serving as a junior minister, he was made a Baronet. In 1974 he was given a Life Peerage, and from 1979 to 1984 served as an MEP for Manchester South. Not bad going for a lad who was born above a pub in Darlaston, West Midlands! Away from politics his other great passion was the theatre. At one time he was on the boards of Stoll Moss Empires and Radio Luxemburg, and was also Chairman of the Malvern Festival Trust.

He was also a champion of provincial theatre, and a life-long patron of the Grand Theatre Wolverhampton, where he and his wife used to go almost every Saturday night. His other great love was variety, and when in London was often to be found at the old Player's Theatre underneath the arches at Charing Cross, where the great tradition of Victorian Music Hall still flourishes. He was also a wonderful raconteur, with a fund of hilarious stories which he would regale us with over Sunday lunch. His appearance at Sunday lunch was something I always looked forward to. All week he would dress in the manner befitting a man of his years and high position in life, sober-suited, and with a proper sense of decorum and sartorial elegance.

But for some reason on Sundays he would come down from his bedroom arrayed in a motley collection of garments, which he called his 'casual look'. I remember one Sunday he appeared wearing a shapeless pair of brown corduroy trousers, which ended above his ankles, a canary-yellow shirt, a paisley patterned neckerchief and a loud-check waistcoat; which made him look rather like one of the villagers in an amateur production of The Barber of Seville. He *was* rather eccentric, but I sometimes got the feeling that he was putting it on a bit, and that he enjoyed incurring the wrath of his long-suffering wife and daughters. I liked and admired him enormously; and I think he was quite fond of me. Sadly, within a year, Sue's mother had died; and another service of remembrance was held at St. Andrew's, the village church In Weston; where, once again, I was asked to write and to read a tribute to my dear mother-in-law; which I did gladly.

Old theatrical joke:
What's the difference between Laurence Olivier and Donald Wolfit? Laurence Olivier is a *tour de force*; and Donald Wolfit is forced to tour! Ha, ha.

Touring, now there's something I never really cared for. I know it's a great theatrical tradition dating back to Shakespearean times, the strolling players and all that, but lugging a suitcase full of dirty washing from one dreary northern town to another while scanning the digs list for somewhere cheap to stay, never appealed to me, even when I was younger. However, lots of actors do like it, and some even enjoy it. Kate O'Mara being one of them.

Back in the 1970s Kate was a family friend, known to us as 'The girl with a flat full of dead plants' because she was away on tour so often. We only worked together once and that, oddly enough, was on a tour. I remember that at every theatre we played Kate's dressing room would immediately become a miniature home-from-home. There would be a crisp, lace-edged cloth on her dressing table, upon which were placed a vase of fresh flowers and countless bottles of lotions and potions, hair sprays and perfumes. Good luck cards were pinned up all around the mirror, and photos and mementos dotted around the room with, here and there, a colourful piece of cloth draped over a chair or sofa.

By contrast, my dressing room looked like a prison cell, with just a box of Kleenex, a roll-on deodorant, a bar of soap and a towel.
I didn't mind the pre-London tours, even though in my case some never made it to the West End, and those that did soon folded because there was something to look forward to at the end of the journey. But traipsing around the country in a creaky old potboiler of a play and then signing on at the Labour Exchange, was not my idea of *la dolce vita*.

Whenever I did go out on tour I always made a point of getting to know the stage-door keeper, buying him a can of beer occasionally, and tipping him when I left. If nothing else it ensured that any phone messages would be passed on to you immediately.

Before the advent of mobile phones it was the stage-door keeper's phone that was the lifeline when you were on tour, the only connection to friends and family in London but, more importantly, to your agent.

Stage-door keepers are an odd bunch. Some of them have been at their posts for many years. After a while, because they are in daily contact with a succession of famous actors and actresses, they *can* become a bit blasé. A case in point being the Stage-door keeper at the Palace theatre Manchester who, when told that Alan Bennett's play *Forty Years On* was coming to the theatre on its pre-London tour with Sir John Gielgud in the lead, said: "John Gielgud? Even Ken Dodd couldn't fill this place."

In the Aldwych theatre in SW London there is a dressing room on the first floor with a second door, which leads out onto an emergency exit staircase. The door was not part of the original building, it was put in at a later date. But by whom and what was it for? Throughout the 1920s and 30s the Aldwych was the home of farce and Tom Walls, Ralph Lynn, Robertson Hare and Yvonne Arnaud virtually took up residence there. Although they were all experienced *farceurs*, it was

Tom Walls who was the star, producing and directing many of the farces that were shown there over the years.

He was also a film director, and owned (and trained) several racehorses one of whom, April the Fifth, won the Derby in 1935. It was in his dressing room that the door was situated, and it was he who had it put in, telling his wife that it was an escape rout in case of fire. The story goes that Tom Walls was a philanderer given to entertaining ladies in his dressing room between shows on matinee days, and after the shows at night. However his wife, perhaps aware of her husband's roving eye, would often turn up at the stage door at different times, unannounced, and go straight up to his dressing room.

Although the stage-door keeper would hastily ring Mr Walls on the internal phone link, it still occasioned Tom several narrow squeaks, in scenes, I imagine, not unlike those he was appearing in every night on stage! To counteract the surprise element of his wife's visits Tom, ever resourceful, had a warning bell rigged up; with the button in the stage-door keeper's office, and the bell fixed, out of sight, to the underside of his dressing table giving him valuable seconds in which to dispose of the 'evidence'. And so it was that normal service was resumed. The stage-door keeper was no doubt rewarded for his pains, and the *liaisons* continued; perhaps not quite so *dangereux* as they were before.

In July 1995 Sue, our friend Peter Baldwin and myself were invited to join the QE2 as guest speakers for the five day trip to New York. None of us had ever been on a ship of that size before, or been at sea for that length of time, so it promised to be a unique experience. Our cabins were luxurious, the cuisine in both restaurants was first class, and the wine list extensive, so we were set fair for our voyage to the Big Apple. As we got under way we discovered that the majority of passengers on board were American and, of course, had never heard of Coronation Street. Consequently we only did one question-and-answer talk show in the ship's theatre instead of the agreed two. Feeling that perhaps we hadn't fully repaid Cunard for their hospitality, Peter offered to do his one-man show 'Oscar Wilde'.

With great prescience he had packed his wig, velvet jacket and floppy bow tie; and gave a wonderful show to a packed and appreciative audience. On our third night at sea we were invited to join the Captain in his cabin for pre-prandial drinks. When we arrived there were around a dozen people being served drinks by two stewards. Looking around, the first person I saw was that fine American film actor, Ned Beatty. Then, no sooner had I got over the initial surprise of seeing such a well known movie actor in close-up, as it were; I realised that the man standing talking to the Captain was none other than *Gene Hackman*! In my opinion Gene Hackman is among the top ten film actors in the world right now, with Ned Beatty not far behind. Upon seeing us the Captain excused himself and came over to greet us. When he had moved on Sue, knowing how much I admired Gene Hackman, said "Now's your chance. Go over and introduce yourself." But for some reason I was reluctant to do so. I don't know why, but I felt that it was being, well, a bit pushy. Having no such qualms herself, my darling wife grabbed my arm and dragged me over to where Gene Hackman was now chatting to his wife. "Hello," she said. "My name is Sue Eden and this is my husband, Mark. He is an actor himself, and a great admirer of your work." We shook hands, Gene Hackman introduced us to his wife, and we chatted amiably for a few minutes before moving on to introduce ourselves to Ned Beatty and his wife, who were both charming. Isn't it always the way? You wait ages to meet a big American movie star then – like the number 31 London bus – two come along together!

On the morning of our arrival in New York we got up at 5am especially to see the sun rise behind the Manhattan skyline. It was a wonderful sight with the skyscrapers in shadow, silhouetted against a roseate sky.

We stayed at the famous Algonquin Hotel on West 44th Street where, in the 1920's and 30's Dorothy Parker, Robert Benchley, Alexander Woollcott et al, held court at the Round Table, dubbing themselves The Vicious Circle. Whereas on my previous trip to New

York I had been working (shooting two commercials for TWA) this time I was a tourist and every morning, guide book in hand, we 'did' New York. We saw a Broadway show (How to Succeed in Business – Without Really Trying) and rubbernecked or way around all the major places of interest in New York returning to London, by air, on the 31st of July. If you've never been to New York, go there. It's a great city.

CHAPTER 23

THE LOVELIEST AND THE BEST

On June 6th 2003, 41 days after her 100th birthday, my beloved mother died. She had been determined to celebrate her centenary *and* receive a message from the Queen, and she did. The fact that she had lived long enough to achieve both ambitions was due, in no small part, to her innate tenacity and in the larger part to the care and devotion of my sister Kathleen on whom, in the last five years of her life, she became totally dependent. Kathleen had given up full-time work to look after her in her own home.

She did it willingly and gladly, knowing how much mum dreaded ending up in a care home. Helped by my brother Chas, they brought love, reassurance and peace of mind to my mother's final years. On the day of her funeral we had a requiem mass said for her at St. Dominic's Priory where mum had worshiped for so long. All the surviving members of our extended family were there, along with Polly, Saul and ex wife Diana, and we laid her to rest next to my father and brother Eddie in Finchley Cemetery.

I began these memoirs with the first two lines of a John Masefield poem and, in a tribute to my dear mother, here it is in full.

In the dark womb where I began
My mother's life made me a man.
Through all the months of human birth
Her beauty fed my common earth.
I cannot see, nor breathe, nor stir,
But through the death of some of her.
Down in the darkness of the grave

She cannot see the life she gave.
For all her love, she cannot tell
Whether I use it ill or well,
Nor knock the dusty doors to find
Her beauty dusty in the mind.
If the grave's gates could be undone,
She would not know her little son,
I am so grown, if we should meet,
She would pass by me in the street,
Unless my soul's face let her see
My sense of what she did for me.

What have I done to keep in mind
My debt to her and womankind?
What woman's happier life repays
Her for those months of wretched days?
For all my mouth less body leech'd
Ere Birth's releasing hell was reach'd?
What have I done, or tried, or said
In thanks to that dear woman dead?
Men triumph over women still,
Men trample women's rights at will,
And man's lust roves the world untamed.
O grave, keep shut lest I be shamed.
RIP.

One night in late September 2006 I received a phone call from Tom Bell. I thought at the time he sounded a bit strange, but put it down to him 'having had the drink taken', not an unusual occurrence for Tom.

There appeared to be no particular reason for the call; we reminisced about our time together in rep at Swansea Grand, and all the good times we'd had over the years. Then he said: "I love talking to you, Mark, cos you make me laugh. Ta-ra, love,", and put down the 'phone.

On October 5th Sue and I were in Sitges in Spain having dinner in our hotel when Sue received a text message from my ex wife Diana. It read: "Sorry to be the bearer of sad tidings. Tom Bell died yesterday. Thought you'd like to know."

As soon as we returned to London I phoned Tom's partner, Frances Tempest. She told me that Tom had been in hospital for four weeks prior to his death (from pneumonia) which meant that he must have phoned me that night from his hospital bed – and never mentioned it to me. I went down to Brighton for the cremation and placed a sunflower on his coffin. He was 73.

Then, in the December of the following year I had a phone call from my friend Stewart Permutt, to tell me that my dear friend Ken Parry had died as the result of a heart attack at his home in Islington. Because the Festive Season was already under way, the church Kenny had selected for his funeral service was fully booked up so his cremation was postponed until January 2008.

Sadly, I was up in Manchester at the time and, once again, the train services to London were severely disrupted; so I didn't get to the service. Kenny once told me that he wanted his gravestone to read: "Ken Parry. Actor. Pissed and passed on!" Somehow, I don't think he got his wish.

"I grow old...I grow old... I shall wear the bottoms of my trousers rolled."

It is now 2010. My 82nd birthday has come and gone. In July of this year Sue and I will have been together for 27 years, so we must be doing something right. We each give love and support to the other, and still make each other laugh; very important, that. I still cannot believe my good fortune. At the age of 56, with two failed marriages behind me, I met the love of my life. How lucky is that? I cannot imagine my life without her.

On Saturday August 28th 2004 my stepson Saul married the lovely Theresa Kelly, and almost a year later on Friday August 19th 2005 my darling Polly married her long-term boyfriend, the handsome Alex Wrenn.

Since then Saul and Theresa have had three children: twins Ned and Jude and little Lola, and Alex and Polly have produced two delightful little boys, Freddie and Ronnie; which means that, along with my son David's actress daughter Emma, I now have six grandchildren! So I consider myself twice blessed.

Sometimes, when sleep eludes me - increasingly so of late - I cast my mind back over my life. A life not *entirely* wasted, as it might so easily have been. Some hopes fulfilled, others yet to be realised.

There is still time!

I shall let Edward Fitzgerald have the final word with an extract from one of my favourite poems; his epic translation of The Rubaiyat of Omar Khayyam; the man who, in these four stanzas, sums up the final chapter of our lives.

> *'Ah, my beloved, fill the cup that clears*
> *Today of past regrets and future fears –*
> *Tomorrow? – Why tomorrow I may be*
> *Myself with Yesterday's Sev'n Thousand years.*
>
> *Lo! Some we loved, the loveliest and the best*
> *That Time and Fate of all their vintage prest,*
> *Have drunk their Cup a Round or two before,*
> *And one by one crept silently to Rest.*
>
> *And we, that now make merry in the Room*
> *They left, and Summer dresses in new Bloom,*
> *Ourselves must we beneath the Couch of Earth*
> *Descend, ourselves to make a Couch – for whom?*
>
> *Ah, make the most of what we yet may spend,*
> *Before we too into the Dust descend;*
> *Dust into Dust, and under Dust to lie,*
> *Sans Wine, sans Song, sans Singer, and – sans End!*

Well, perhaps not *quite* the final word; there is just one last thing I want to say before I sign off.

It is in answer to my dear old mum's oft-quoted put-down whenever she thought I was getting 'a bit above myself'; and which gave me the title for my autobiography – Who's going to look at *you*?

Impossible to say for certain, mum; but in just *two* of my episodes of Coronation Street alone we had an audience of over fifty million! So over 50 Years? Worldwide? Oh, at least a billion people I would think. And that's a conservative estimate!

EXIT STAGE LEFT. HANDS IN POCKETS. WHISTLING.

CURTAIN.

ENDPIECE.

On August 3, 2009 at exactly 3.27pm my brother Charlie died at the Marie Curie Hospice in Belsize Park, London. He was 79. He had battled long and hard for life but, as with most cancers, it was a desperately uneven struggle. In our childhood I had taken care of him, in our teens I had kept a brotherly eye on him, and I was with him at the end.

His was a life in which he never enjoyed robust good health, and seemed to have rather more than his fair share of misfortunes but it was a life full of kindness and amiability.

Spurred on perhaps by my example, he became an actor. After studying drama at the Mountview Theatre School, he spent several seasons at various repertory companies including Ayr, Crewe, Ventnor IOW and Swansea (where I began my career) and became an excellent character actor. But after a couple of years reluctantly decided that the insecure life of an actor was not for him and became a London taxi-cab driver.

When he was diagnosed with cancer of the oesophagus he was stoical about it; and never complained throughout his long illness.Once again my dear sister, Kathleen, looked after him at home until it became necessary for him to go into a hospice. From then on she sat with him all day, every day, tending his needs until the end. No one could have had more loving care than my brother and no one deserved it more than he. My sister Kathleen is a saintly woman and, if there *is* a Heaven, along with my dear mother, has most surely attained her place within its fabled pearly gates.

Charles William Malin was a good man: modest, gentle, considerate and generous. He will be sorely missed.

Index